WILDLY INSPIRED

TAP THE CREATIVE POWER OF NATURE

JONI SENSEL

dream factory
DREAM FACTORY BOOKS

Dedicated to the creative spirit in nature and all people—including you.

Copyright © 2025 Joni Sensel
All rights reserved.
Reproduction or distribution of any part of this book without permission is prohibited.
Personal, noncommercial, or classroom use is permitted with proper credit to the author and source.
Published in the United States by Dream Factory Books
Enumclaw, WA

Library of Congress Control Number: 2025917410

Cover & icons: Dana J. Sullivan
All images © Joni Sensel unless otherwise noted.

ISBN: 978-0-9701195-9-9

Welcome

Want to feed your creativity, helping it flow more freely? Need help weathering the storms of daily life that can otherwise derail creative projects or crush creativity altogether? Long to strengthen your connection to the natural world *and* the fertile powers that bubble inside?

This book is for you. Welcome to a more creative life.

Praise for Wildly Inspired

"As I sit here, Fall is arriving. A new season! Which means new energy, new hope, and new possibilities. Connect your creative spirit to nature and to the changing seasons with Joni Sensel's new book *Wildly Inspired*. Highly recommended!"

—Eric Maisel, *Brave New Mind* and 60+ books

"In *Wildly Inspired*, Joni Sensel takes readers deep inside their creative selves to partner with the power of nature. Sensel's clear and simple guidance leads creative seekers to unearth brand new territory holding fresh perspectives and original material. The book is invaluable to anyone aiming for excellence in their creative expression. So get the book and be *Wildly Inspired* yourself."

—Tina Welling, author of *Writing Wild*

"An original and fascinating way of expanding creativity through our experiences in the natural world, complete with detailed explanations and multiple guided exercises. Highly recommended for writers seeking new avenues, via the natural world, to reach creative insight, both for personal artistic growth and for enriching specific writing projects."

—Janet Fox, award-winning author and writing coach

"I am over the moon about *Wildly Inspired*! Imagine dazzling sunshine awakening your creativity from a deep winter into an unexpected spring. Joni Sensel is our worthy mentor in this fresh-and-ancient, wildly inspiring guide that lives up to its name."

—Deb Lund, creativity coach, author, and environmental educator

A note about my sources

My personal exploration of the concepts in this book began in earnest through courses in the "Four Shields" model of human development expounded in the 1990s by Stephen Foster and Meredith Little and later extended by Bill Plotkin in books such as *Nature and the Human Soul*. Foster and Little's lengthy book on the subject, *The Four Shields: The Initiatory Seasons of Human Nature*, acknowledged its Native American sources, but unfortunately those inspirations were not well credited and were removed from their cultural contexts.

However, I agree with Foster, Little, and Plotkin that the ideas capture enduring human truths that transcend cultures. This conclusion is supported by ideas incorporated here from the work of anthropologist Arnold van Gennep, comparative mythologist and author Joseph Campbell, psychologist Carl G. Jung, educator and author Parker J. Palmer, ecopsychologist Craig Chalquist, and theologian Matthew Fox, among others.

This book reflects my synthesis of these ideas specifically as they apply to creativity. It's my effort to share a perspective I've found valuable with readers who are otherwise unlikely to encounter the concepts in the thriving but limited ways they're currently practiced elsewhere—including in specific cultural applications.

Contents

Author's Note: A Gift from the Dawn 1

PART 1: A New Way to Grow Your Creativity 5

Chapter 1: Nature Is Creativity on Display 7
    The Creative Critter's Shopping Spree 8

Chapter 2: Why Map Creativity to the Seasons? 13
    The Seasonal Cycle of the Hero's Journey 17
    The Seasonal Cycle of the Artist's Journey 19
    Seasonal Energy Tendencies 20

Chapter 3: Exploring the Energies of Each Season 25
    Fire, Water, Spikes, and Wings 28
    Speaking of Journeys: Archetypes 32

Chapter 4: Whose Season Is It, Anyway? 37
    Define Your Own Seasons 40

Chapter 5: How to Use This Workbook from Here 41
    Part 1 Endnotes *49*

PART 2: Putting the Seasons to Work 53

Spark New Creation in Spring 55
    Find a Project Talisman 59
    Step over a Threshold 61
    Conspire with Clouds 64
    Connect with Your Artistic Spirit 66
    Capture Sounds on Sticky Notes 68
    Cross-Pollinate 70
    Break a Rule 75
    Open the Door 76
    Explore Voice with Birdsong 78

Think Divergently 80
Inhale and Exhale to Create 83
Sweep Clean 86
Spring Endnotes *89*

Embody Summer 91
Identify Your Creative Element 95
Praise Your Hands 98
Shed Your Shoes 99
Let Your Body Inspire You 101
Go on a Symbolic Thinking Scavenger Hunt 103
Explore Your Psychic Landscape 105
Ask for a Sign 108
Find a Familiar 111
Map Your Passion 113
See Yourself as a Tree 115
Create an Earth Altar 117
Rely on Your Wrong Hand 119
Summer Endnotes *121*

Fall Inward 125
Examine Your Plate 129
Release What's No Longer Useful 131
Ebb and Flow 133
Connect with Water 135
Flavor Your Work 137
Catch Reflections 139
Go Deeper with Five Whys 141
Unearth Secrets 143
Indulge in Ideas 145
Befriend Your Monster 147
Trick Out Your Tombstone 150
Decipher Wild Writing 152
Autumn Endnotes *156*

Embrace Winter's Wisdom 159
Picture This 163
Take Stock with a Snowflake 165

Gnaw Your Creative Bone 168
Expose Something Hiding 170
Find Shelter (but Avoid Cages) 173
Strengthen Roots by Mining Memories 175
Rest with the Rain 178
Practice Resilience with Rocks 180
Step into a Story 182
Acknowledge Loss 184
Sidle up to Storytellers 186
Build a Better Vision Board 189
Shine Light on Deceptions 192
Fracture Your Own Fairy Tale 195
Winter Endnotes *199*

Spiral Forward **203**

Author's Note: A Gift from the Dawn

This book is a gift from the rising sun.

I had crawled from my warm tent before 5 a.m. to catch the dawn over Colorado's Sangre de Christo mountains. When I woke, stars still dotted the heavens—a welcome sight, since wildfire smoke had choked off the blue for days, leaving the sky an ominous orange. Now I could hope for a real sunrise, not merely a ruddy glow.

I rose early that morning to seek inspiration. Several days of retreat in the mountains had confirmed a decision half-made in my heart for months: I was setting aside publication goals I'd carried for more than a decade.

Though I'd published six novels for young readers—five through traditional methods and another via self-publishing—I'd subsequently spent too many years without much success. At last I was resolved to take the hint, to stop beating my head against a market that wasn't interested in the stories I had to tell.

But where to focus my creative energy instead? I didn't know. So that morning, I crept through the darkness and up a rock-littered slope to await the first rays of the sun. Perhaps I'd be granted an inspiration about how to spend my newly freed time.

As you'll see in the pages to come, I had reason to hope for a bolt of insight from the East. I've spent much of my life outdoors: hiking, camping, and scuba diving, turning the trees and the cliffs, the fish and the squirrels, into friends. Nature has so often inspired me: ideas for novels, plot points, settings, and characters. I seek signs in nature and seem to find them.

I rose early that morning to seek inspiration.

It has long been apparent to me that nature speaks to us, if we learn how to listen. Three of my novels rely on this notion. Their characters understand the soft voices of trees and can hear the grumbling wisdom of stones.

But fiction is not real life. So as I crouched on a shadowy boulder, huddled into a blanket against the altitude's chill, I didn't know what might come. I simply tried to be open—to animal silhouettes in the gloom, the sweet scent of an unfamiliar bush to my right, the tentative chirping of invisible birds.

I also mused my question about what to do next. What kind of work might readers embrace? Well, what many want most is help creating their own stories and art. That's true both of people who identify as creative and of many who are privately convinced they are not. Maybe I could offer such help. But I didn't have any success secrets, did I? If I did, more of my books would exist between covers instead of merely as digital files.

In fact, more than a year before, a friend had suggested I write a creativity book. I lead workshops on the topic and have a fascination for the imagination, which not only helps us express who we are but connects us with a greater, divine generative force. But I couldn't figure out how to approach such a book or set it apart from those that already exist. I'd quickly dismissed the idea and hadn't given it much more thought. Not until that week in the mountains.

The sky slowly paled. The shadows grew thin. I waited for the sun to appear. It seemed to be lagging. The details of wildflowers and lichen around me were plain. Yet the brightest spot over the ridge to my east had yet to produce golden rays.

I watched that glow on the horizon, anticipating. As the sun broke the rim and rays dazzled my eyes, the answer to my question arrived in my mind: Present nature as a portal to creativity. I could pull together all the ways I used the natural environment as a pathway to creative work.

Thank you, great sun!

> *As the sun broke the rim and rays dazzled my eyes, the answer to my question arrived in my mind.*

Author's Note: A Gift from the Dawn

Once revealed, it seemed obvious. The possibilities and implications ricocheted through my mind. It's common to think of creativity as something we strive for while alone at an easel or desk, when it's actually an energy flowing to enliven the Earth. The creative force is expressed broadly through nature in everything from the astonishing diversity of flower blossoms to the sometimes wacky behavior of humans with time on their hands. In my opinion, there's no better way to access it than to connect with that natural world.

© istock.com/vovik_mar

What's more, I'd spent the last several days talking with a small group of people about how Earth's seasons are reflected in the stages and challenges of our lives, from childhood to old age. Now, I abruptly recognized a similar cycle in the inception, development, completion, and release of ideas and creative works. I could draw on all these connections to share my creativity techniques, and I could structure the collection around the four seasons. The resulting book might spark ideas for others, as the sun sparked this one for me. It might even nudge readers closer to the Earth and the natural energies that course through us all.

Both delighted by this idea and daunted, I got to work. Whenever I faltered, the Earth got me moving again. At last, after seasons of heated activity and others of cool doubt and rest, I offer this book. (If I could, I'd arrange for you to find it under a tree.) It offers techniques for accessing the creative fire of nature and setting those flames alight within you.

It's common to think of creativity as something we strive for while alone at an easel or desk, when it's actually an energy flowing to enliven the Earth.

In a sense, this book takes you on your own creativity retreat, but not to a dawn-gilded wilderness peak. Instead, the wilderness we'll explore together is the *anima mundi,* the soul of the natural world.[1] Wilderness experiences can transform lives, in part because they remove us from habitual routines to reveal new perspectives. But it can be difficult to act on the insights received. The return to everyday life, to laundry and traffic, triggers old habits.

This book takes a more integrated approach, offering activities to try as part of your usual creative practice or as small steps to building a new one. When your habits and responsibilities remain all around you, smaller doses of insight can squeeze in through the cracks and persist. In that way, this book can transform your creativity over time from within the constraints of your daily routines. In addition, reconnecting with nature can help counteract the stress of our high-tech daily lives—and while there are exceptions, stress is generally acknowledged as a creativity blocker[2] worth fighting.

Don't worry. I'm not suggesting you rise before dawn or trek into the woods unless that's what you're called to do. Nature is as close as your backyard, a park, the houseplant on your windowsill, and your own precious body. It's waiting 24 hours a day to be noticed. This book won't push you to physical or emotional limits, but it will push you to try things you haven't before. You'll take concrete steps toward creating more originally, joyfully, and productively. And you'll explore powerful tools that can help you build a more connected, more fulfilling creative practice that's more grounded in your environment, your deepest self, and your soul.

I hope this book can be a gift for you, too.

This book can transform your creativity over time from within the constraints of your daily routines.

PART 1:

A New Way to Grow Your Creativity

Chapter 1:
Nature Is Creativity on Display

At its most basic level, creativity is the life force that prompts a seed to sprout and grow roots, stems, leaves, and fruit, creating a tree where no tree stood before. Our planet is ridiculously creative—consider the fantastic varieties of insects or undersea life or the beautiful formations of mineral crystals and snowflakes. It's hard to spend much time observing the natural world without thinking of Ma Nature as promiscuously creative, exploding into variety simply because she can. For the pure joy of it.

By more intentionally connecting with this rambunctious force—which blazes both around and within you—you can grow and expand your own creativity, no matter how you express it. The seasons are a worthy map for this exploration, and this book is intended to both guide you and help document your journey through a year (or more) of creative play, experimentation, and growth. We'll set your creative spirit loose into its native environment and follow where it leads. You'll come back transformed.

So turn the page, and let's go!

By more intentionally connecting with this rambunctious force, you can grow and expand your own creativity.

The Creative Critter's Shopping Spree

How this can help you: Kick off the playful mindset that promotes creativity, engage both verbal and visual parts of the brain to encourage new connections, and begin mining the metaphorical language of the subconscious.

Imagine you're a small, soft-bodied creature about to embark on a big new adventure. You're in line at Gaia's Gear Mart to choose the clothing and equipment you want to wear and take with you. It's hard to say where your travels will take you, but you'll figure it out as you go. Happily, budget's no issue. There are so many choices! But nature's not stingy. How you combine them? That's creativity. Welcome to the Creative Critter's Shopping Spree.

Select one from each row. Don't overthink it; just choose. Then total your selections in each column. If you're reluctant to write in this book, copy these two pages instead.

1. I'll wear a coat made of:	☐ Feathers	☐ Scales	☐ Shell	☐ Fur
2. I'll also take a supply of protective:	☐ Cocoon silk	☐ Quills	☐ Slime	☐ Bony plates
3. From the skills rack, I'll choose:	☐ Sharp hearing	☐ Navigation	☐ A keen nose	☐ Radar
4. Since they're on sale, I'll take a few extra:	☐ Hearts	☐ Legs	☐ Stomachs	☐ Eyes
5. I can also use:	☐ A pair of wings	☐ A horn or two	☐ A pair of fins	☐ A long tail
6. For confidence in any situation, I'll take:	☐ Speed	☐ Agility	☐ Camouflage	☐ Strength
7. In case things get rough, I'll also bring:	☐ Talons	☐ A stinger	☐ Poison	☐ Fangs
8. If I find companions, I'll:	☐ Pull tricks on them	☐ Play with them	☐ Hide & spy on them	☐ Help them
9. To communicate, I will:	☐ Whistle	☐ Drum	☐ Rattle	☐ Howl
10. I plan to travel by:	☐ Hopping	☐ Running	☐ Drifting	☐ Tunneling
11. If a road romance blooms, I'll impress with my:	☐ Beauty	☐ Humor	☐ Kisses	☐ Brains
12. If I get time, I might stop by:	☐ Paris	☐ Cairo	☐ Venice	☐ Iceland
13. I especially hope my adventures will take me to:	☐ Heaven	☐ Middle Earth	☐ Atlantis	☐ Home again

Total for each column:

Next, before we assess your choices, take a whack at drawing the creature you've built.

I'm not kidding. Colored pencils or crayons will make it more fun. Here's mine, a sort of flying, spiked tribble. You can see that drawing ability doesn't matter—and remember, a willingness to occasionally look foolish is a crucial component of creative breakthroughs.

Draw your critter below. Give it a name if you like.

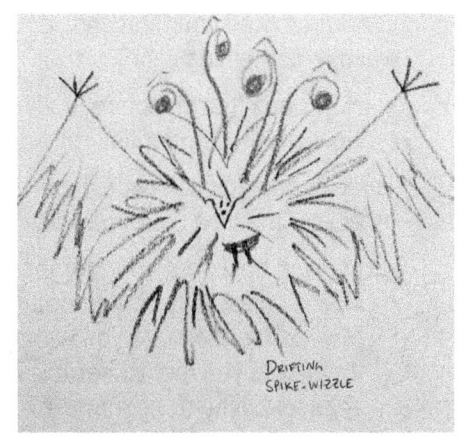

My Creative Critter

Does this seem like random silliness? It's not. We'll use your answers in several ways. For starters, they can help you explore half-buried attitudes and motivations that may underlie your creative choices.

Answer the following questions about your shopping spree choices. Use a journal if you'd like space to write and reflect. You'll want one for many of the activities in this book anyhow.

- What prompted your first choice, which was for a coat? Aesthetics, durability, comfort, whimsy, something else?
  - How does that choice reflect your priorities generally?
  - How are those priorities reflected in your creative work?
- Three shopping spree questions—2, 6, and 7—get directly at issues of danger and defense. Question 5 can be related, too. How did those questions make you feel?
  - Looking back, are your defenses aimed more at standing your ground or escaping?
  - How aggressively do you defend your art-making time or your own vision?
  - How comfortable are you with marketing or promoting your work? Do promotional activities make you feel vulnerable? Are you poised to retreat? Or do you worry about being seen as pushy or aggressive? Are you?
- Question 9, on communication, has direct bearing on your art. How might your choice be a metaphor for how you feel about it? *(For instance, do you feel unrecognized, howling alone in the darkness? Or is your creative work a way to "beat a drum" on a particular message?)*
  - If this question makes you uncomfortable or your answer seems "wrong," what noise-making metaphor would you prefer to associate with your art? Why that one?
- Question 8, about companions, might reveal hidden attitudes toward your creative community. How does your answer hint at how competitive, collaborative, or alone you feel?
- Question 13 carries implications about goals and values. How does your answer relate to your creative work or themes you explore? Is there another choice you'd prefer?
- Look back at your drawing and compare it with the choices you made. Which features are the most prominent in your drawing? What associations do you have with those features? *(For instance, my critter's wild fur speaks to me of warmth and comfort, while wings make me think both of escape and wild flights of fancy.)*
  - How do those associations resonate in your work or emotional life? *(To continue with my example, the quills and fangs in my drawing were afterthoughts, perhaps because I don't think of myself or my work as very biting or dangerous, and in a conflict I'm more likely to fly away than attack.)*
- Now that you know this quiz was a bit more than a lark, how do you feel about it? *(For instance, do you feel tricked, entertained, or intrigued?)*
  - What hidden traits may have surfaced in you, such as a streak of perfectionism, a need for control, a tendency toward overanalysis, or a sense of whimsy?
- Finally, if you're a writer or other kind of storyteller, you might go back and try shopping again from the point of view of the main character in your current project. Consider the questions above from their perspective, too. It can be useful to see how your own answers align with or diverge from those of your protagonist.

The Creative Critter questions have no right answers. They're not scientific. They simply provoke you to think more metaphorically than you normally may. Many of the activities in this book will do that. Since the subconscious speaks largely through metaphor and image, such activities can help you unearth attitudes and ideas that are buried beneath your conscious awareness. Bringing them to the surface can help you express them in ways that support your creative goals.

If your eyebrows are raised already, let me warn you: This book includes psychological concepts that some might consider esoteric or "woo-woo." While many creative people find them effective, you needn't believe anything. Just try the activities to see if they stir your creative energies in playful and productive ways. As with critical feedback and everything else intended to support your creativity, take what resonates and leave the rest.

We'll return to this Creative Critter activity and how it relates to the seasons shortly. In the meantime, I hope you've begun feeling playful and considered the idea that, as with T.S. Eliot's conception of the literary device known as the objective correlative,[3] the natural world around us can reflect our inner lives. That's why honing your awareness of nature's creativity can help you explore and develop your own.

"I went out for a walk and finally concluded to stay out till sundown, for going out, I found, was really going in." —John Muir

The next chapter explains why seasons matter to creative work, especially for artists and storytellers. It includes a fun questionnaire that will help you identify which seasonal energies you might need help with.

If you've read enough for now, however, turn instead to an activity for the season you're in and try it. Or, if the

Such activities can help you unearth attitudes and ideas that are buried beneath your conscious awareness.

shopping spree primed your imagination, go channel that energy into your work. After all, that's the ultimate goal. Chapter 2 and its seasonal self-assessment will be waiting for you when you're ready.

Chapter 2:
Why Map Creativity to the Seasons?
(Hint: Because your body and subconscious already do)

We live on a planet that leans. It's tipped on its north/south axis as it orbits the sun. That means some parts of the Earth tilt toward the sun while others lean away from it—and vice versa. The parts that lean toward the sun receive more direct solar rays, making them warmer and giving them more daylight compared with the places that are tipped away. As the Earth circles the sun over a year, the basking part and the chilly part alternate. For the lucky parts in the middle—the tropics—the difference is slight and noticed mostly in wet and dry cycles.

Prehistoric people tracked these changes as they watched animal migrations, plant growth, and the heavens. Early farmers relied on them to know the best times for planting and harvest. Some ancient calendars, including the Old Norse, considered only two seasons, summer and winter. Others focused on the lunar months and specific associations with each. But at least since Roman times, the four seasons have been known consistently in Western cultures as winter, spring, summer, and harvest, later called autumn. Ancient people in the East recognized essentially the same seasons, though some identified five seasons rather than four. (The fifth was often the soggy time of monsoons during late summer.)

Humans share common associations with each season that are rooted in the cycles of life and death all around us.

A season for stories

My own earliest memories related to the seasons were formed when I was four years old. I learned to read with a

P.D. Eastman and Roy McKie picture book called *Snow*. Somehow the black letters on the book's white pages—which I could name in alphabet order but not rearrange—connected with the white snowflakes that fell from the sky. I understood in a flash that just as I could press white snowflakes together into snowballs and snowmen and snow forts, the black letters could be lumped together to form different words. And a lump formed of s-n-o-w meant snow.

Snow didn't fall often in the Pacific Northwest where I lived. Rain was a more common guest. But rain couldn't be shaped into sculptures or igloos, and it dripped all year around. Spell it b-o-r-i-n-g. Snow, more delightful, appeared only in winter. That made winter special. And perfect for reading stories.

Ever since that day, for me the seasons have been linked with words, stories, reading, and writing, and therefore creativity. I'm not alone. Across cultures, humans share common associations with each season that are rooted in our dependence on Earth for our food and in the cycles of life and death all around us.

How seasons echo through our psyches

Spring fling. May/December romance. Even "the winter of our discontent." Such idioms suggest our intuitive awareness of specific seasonal associations that have been deeply ingrained in our hearts, minds, and psyches—if not our genes—through mythology, religion, and other traditions. This is because the seasons provide potent metaphors for universal aspects of experience: The fertility and new life that mark spring; the wild growth, blooming, and ripening of summer; the harvests, transformations, and impending death that loom over autumn; and the loss, hard times, and turning inward of winter.

In fact, the cycle of seasons is an archetype, a subconscious template for change. It's so fundamental to our lives that it's often used as a map for human development. Spring represents

> *The cycle of seasons is an archetype, a subconscious template for change.*

birth; summer celebrates the flourishing of childhood; autumn evokes adolescence or early maturity; and winter stands for adulthood, responsibility, and aging toward death. As philosopher Gaston Bachelard wrote, "Winter is by far the oldest of the seasons."[4]

We'll explore each season's associations in more detail in Chapter 3. But first consider how the entire cycle echoes across human culture. First, the four-part archetype is so strong that we apply it to other periods of time. The year's quarters, and much of what they represent, also track neatly with the four parts of a day. Dawn corresponds to spring, noon and early afternoon to summer, evening to autumn, and night (especially midnight) to winter. So, too, the four phases of the moon—waxing crescent, full moon, waning crescent, and new (dark) moon. That means that whether we're consciously aware of it or not, we experience the archetypal cycle daily. (Monthly, too, but most modern humans only occasionally notice the moon.)

You don't need to recognize the current phase of the moon for the moods of a season to work in and on you. It's your birthright as a citizen of Earth and a byproduct of the mythology you've absorbed, whether you're aware of those influences or not. We tend to think of ourselves and human society as separate from nature, but as mammals, we're part of and subject to the environment, whether you call it the land, the material universe, or Creation. That's true even where walls and concrete separate us from the dirt and the moss and the rain. We still feel the sun's warmth and the tug of the moon. Our bodies respond to approaching night and temperature cycles in ways that evolved over countless generations.

Our hearts, minds, and creative energies can be influenced by these seasonal cycles more than we realize.

What's more, our hearts, minds, and creative energies can be influenced by these seasonal cycles more than we realize. In fact, a host of research has shown that the season we're born into can have lifelong impacts on both our physical and mental health and our personalities.[5] The activities in this book help you become more aware of those natural influences and leverage them to reduce blocks and help your creativity flow.

Creative work progresses through seasons, too

Like living things, creative works go through a similar cycle of birth, development, ripening, and release (whether to an eager audience or abandonment in a closet). We speak of the germ of an idea, meaning a seed, and might nurse it until it blooms. Critics comment on artistic growth, of work maturing or ripening. Finished works, from movies to video games, are released or "dropped" like ripe fruit or fall leaves. Or perhaps the work only withers and dies. Either way, the artist begins the cycle again, moving on to the next idea or project.

If you've been a writer or artist for long, you know that most individuals are better at some parts of the creative cycle than others—whether that means getting started, finishing, polishing, or attracting audiences. We each resonate with the energies of some seasons more than others, whether as a function of personality, circumstances, environment, or biology.

Culture also plays a role. Our society's current habit is to think about beginnings on January 1, and with that date come new goals, resolutions, or thematic "nudge words." But as researchers know, most of us promptly abandon or forget these new starts.[6] It's hard to "turn over a new leaf" when new leaves won't appear for weeks or months in many climates. Even when they do, most of us aren't capable of mentally focusing on a goal, plan, or theme for a whole year at a time. Daily to-dos get in the way. Unexpected events and ideas derail us. And our interests and attention shift as time passes. That's why experts advise breaking goals into manageable chunks.[7]

> *Creative works go through a similar cycle of birth, development, ripening, and release.*

The seasons are one obvious template to use—and, in fact, much of Western culture has a second important "get started" season: fall's back-to-school vibe. This early social training carries over into adult life when we put away summer's beach reads and turn our attention "back to the grindstone" after Labor Day (of course). Grindstones sharpen and renew tools, an important first step before autumn's harvest and crucial work for ensuring winter survival. Similarly, the fall season marks a shift in energy we apply to longer-term goals. Many of us think, "September already? I'd better get moving on what I wanted to accomplish this year." In addition, the Hebrew calendar marks the Jewish new year, Rosh Hashanah, in late September, providing an alternative fresh start for followers of that tradition. Influences like these, which divide the year into energetic ebbs and flows, are one more reason to consider your creative work using the frame of the seasons.

It's no coincidence that the cycle of seasons can be mapped to the hero's journey.

The seasonal cycle of the hero's journey

Another familiar cycle echoes the seasons—the cycle of the hero's journey, also sometimes known as the mono-myth. Popularized by Joseph Campbell in *The Hero with a Thousand Faces*, this story archetype or pattern is familiar to many writers, filmmakers, and other artists. It's spawned countless books and classes, including Christopher Vogler's *The Writer's Journey*, Steven Pressfield's *The Artist's Journey*, and

THE HERO'S JOURNEY

1. Call to adventure
2. Mentors, allies, and enemies
3. Cross the threshold to the unknown
4. Trials and temptations
5. Face death/the abyss
6. Earn treasure
7. Find the road back
8. Return home reborn to a new role

REINTEGRATION | SEPARATION
THE UNKNOWN

two books called *The Heroine's Journey*, the first of that title by Maureen Murdock.

The cycle of seasons gives structure to the passage of time. The hero's journey does too, since it reflects the basic formula of rites of passage: separation from the community, a dip into the unknown, adventures and trials, and a return to the community in a new role.[8] Scholars have also identified other archetypal cycles associated with this formula, including what's known as the post-heroic journey, but Campbell's traditional hero's journey still holds the most sway. Different renditions of the cycle involve as many as 17 discreet stages, but it can be simplified to a handful. (See the previous page.)

It's no coincidence that the cycle of seasons can be mapped to the hero's journey, with a loss of spring's innocence in summer adventures, hardships in the fall, death in the winter, and rebirth the following spring. Renowned literary critic Northrop Frye even suggested that all literary works—if not all of life—ultimately reflect this seasonal archetype.[9] He mapped the comedies, with their giddy, impulsive spirit, to spring, while romances align with summer. Tragedies, which tell of loss and failure and often end in the hero's death, belong to fall, while the chaos and self-reflectivity of satires fit winter.

Writers don't usually think in these terms, setting out to create a depressing fall book, but that doesn't mean the archetype's not at work. The concept is extended even further in compelling arguments by social critics William Strauss and Neil Howe, who have argued that human societies also pass through predictable, four-part seasonal cycles of expansion, exploration, decay, and crisis.[10] If nothing else, these conceptions illustrate the pervasive power of the seasonal cycle and its many metaphorical applications.

The seasonal cycle of the artist's journey

Part of the power of the hero's journey lies in the fact that we're all the heroes of our own lives. And unless you're new to

Seasonal balance will help you avoid getting stalled on your artistic journey.

your craft, you probably don't need much more than a glance to see how much the artist follows the hero's path. An idea from somewhere mysterious summons the creator to a new project. Mentors and allies offer support through hard times. And most of us eventually confront the abyss, questioning the project, our talent, and our hopes. Fortunately, those who persevere eventually finish the cycle, if not with grand artwork, then at least with the treasure of new skills for the next project.

In that context, I'm calling you to an adventure with the creative energies of the seasons. Keep the hero's journey in mind as you enjoy the activities in this book. It's more obvious in some than in others, but they all support the adventure of an artistic life. They're a stash of magic charms to call on when you're discouraged or stuck. If you're intrigued by the journey itself, check out the titles mentioned above, particularly Vogler's. His insights apply to artists of all kinds and can help motivate you during trials.

Let's plunge in and get more personal. Before we explore how each season might influence your creativity, complete the easy questionnaire that follows. Once you've revealed your own tendencies when it comes to seasonal energy, you can better align your creative habits to bolster any weaknesses and balance them with your strengths.

Why care about balancing your seasonal creative energies? Because as a creative, you are on a journey, and you don't want to get lost before coming back home with your prize. In literary terms, that's the definition of tragedy. Most of us in the modern world find a happy ending—or at least one that's hopeful—more satisfying. That's certainly true for your journey as an artist. Seasonal balance will help you avoid getting stalled on your artistic journey so you can progress through the cycle again and again.

The activities in this book are a stash of magic charms to call on when you're discouraged or stuck.

Wildly Inspired

Seasonal Energy Tendencies

How this can help you: Increase awareness of seasonal energies and their psychological (and a few physiological) associations so you can work toward more balance.

For each question, select one (or at most two) that best match your feelings.

I was born in:	☐ Spring	☐ Summer	☐ Autumn	☐ Winter
I was born at this time of day (if known):	☐ Early morning	☐ Mid-morning to early afternoon	☐ Late afternoon or early evening	☐ Late evening or night
I consider myself:	☐ A morning lark	☐ Best around lunchtime	☐ Best in mid-afternoon	☐ A night owl
My favorite season is:	☐ Spring	☐ Summer	☐ Autumn	☐ Winter
My column(s) with the highest total from the Shopping Spree activity:	☐ First	☐ Second	☐ Third	☐ Fourth
My favorite natural environment:	☐ Meadow	☐ Desert	☐ Forest	☐ Mountains
When I think of my creative work, I realize I sometimes:	☐ Have lots of ideas that don't go anywhere	☐ Start projects but don't always finish	☐ Get things done but then keep them to myself	☐ Churn out the work but take few risks
My favorite color:	☐ Pink, yellow, or lavender	☐ Red, orange, or brown	☐ Green, blue, or purple	☐ Black, white, or grey
I most identify with this creative struggle:	☐ Making time for my art	☐ Focus or follow-through	☐ Discouragement	☐ Losing the joy of the process
On a bad day, it's most likely because I'm:	☐ Anxious	☐ Angry	☐ Sad	☐ Exhausted
Another key challenge for me:	☐ Lack of confidence, imposter syndrome	☐ Reluctance to go to dark or emotional places	☐ Difficulty judging my own work	☐ Working on the same project too long
I most like to sit near this kind of fire:	☐ Birthday candles	☐ Fourth of July sparklers	☐ A bonfire	☐ Fireplace or woodstove
When I make decisions, I rely most on:	☐ Instinct	☐ Practical considerations	☐ Advice, ratings, recommendations	☐ Research and logic
I might call intuition a way of knowing the truth in my:	☐ Soul	☐ Gut	☐ Heart	☐ Bones
On vacation, I love to be:	☐ Learning	☐ Active	☐ Relaxed	☐ Indulgent
Others describe me as:	☐ Inventive	☐ Enthusiastic	☐ Intuitive	☐ Responsible
I'm most likely to struggle with:	☐ Anxiety	☐ Overwhelm	☐ Loneliness	☐ Shame or guilt
Subtotals from this page (how many selected from each column):				

Why Map Creativity to the Seasons?

My favorite secular holiday:	☐ New Year's	☐ My birthday	☐ Halloween	☐ Thanksgiving
I would most like my creative work to be praised as:	☐ Innovative	☐ Playful	☐ Heart-warming	☐ Helpful
I sometimes struggle with:	☐ Distraction: I fall down rabbit holes	☐ Impatience: I share or submit too soon	☐ Perfectionism: My work isn't good enough yet	☐ Workaholism: I need to loosen up
My favorite kind of darkness might be:	☐ A starry night sky	☐ Anywhere I can explore with a flashlight	☐ Behind my closed eyes as I fall asleep	☐ A dark theatre before the show
My biggest creative "guilty pleasure:"	☐ Dreaming: Buying supplies	☐ Keeping up: Studying or enjoying others' art	☐ Community: Talking shop, celebrating	☐ Preparation: Classes, books, workshops
Of these water experiences, I'd choose:	☐ Running through a sprinkler	☐ Rafting a river	☐ Rain drumming on a roof while I'm cozy	☐ Walking in gently falling snow
Of these, I secretly believe the most important for success is:	☐ Luck or timing	☐ Talent	☐ Connections or networking	☐ Hard work
And of these, the most important might be:	☐ Plenty of ideas	☐ Market insight	☐ Emotional awareness	☐ Patience and persistence
The best scent from this list:	☐ Freshly mown grass	☐ A road after rain (petrichor)	☐ Cinnamon	☐ A pine tree
My creative strengths include:	☐ Strong concepts or focal points	☐ Action, rhythm, or movement/plot	☐ Theme, symbolism, or color	☐ Technical proficiency, logic, or details
My top recommendation to newbies who want to get started in the field:	☐ Just dive in and start trying	☐ Immerse yourself in others' work	☐ Take a class	☐ Read a good craft book
In relationships, I admit I can be kind of:	☐ Inconsistent or unreliable	☐ High-maintenance	☐ Withdrawn	☐ Slow to trust
I generally get the most creative work done in:	☐ Spring	☐ Summer	☐ Autumn	☐ Winter
I most relate to this ad slogan:	☐ Think Different	☐ Betcha Can't Eat Just One	☐ Have It Your Way	☐ Just Do It
I can sometimes be:	☐ Absent-minded	☐ Hot-tempered	☐ Gloomy	☐ Lazy
I rely most on:	☐ Action & impulse	☐ Sensations & trial-and-error	☐ Emotions & trends	☐ Facts & systems

Subtotals from this page:

These last five are backed by research on birth seasons:

I'm generally:	☐ Optimistic, even pollyanna-ish	☐ Optimistic but grounded	☐ A realist	☐ A pessimist, though I hate to admit it
I can be subject to:	☐ ADHD symptoms	☐ Quick mood swings	☐ Balanced or flat emotions	☐ Skin problems or food allergies
I'm also:	☐ Often depressed	☐ Irritable	☐ Rarely depressed	☐ Calm and easy-going
My personality tends to be:	☐ Nurturing	☐ Practical or pragmatic	☐ Organized, but caring	☐ Sometimes fanciful
And I am:	☐ A performer or visual artist (maybe secretly)	☐ Better with words than most anything else	☐ Good at math and/or science	☐ Left-handed

Subtotals from this page:

Subtotals from p. 20

Subtotals from p. 21

Add the number in each column for all pages of this questionnaire.

Grand totals:

        Spring   Summer   Autumn   Winter

    Does one season represent a dominant number of your answers? Perhaps more important, which season represents your lowest score?

    The ideal is balance. With that in mind, consider the advice below for whichever season you selected *least* often. With help from the activities that follow, you'll bring more of that season's energies to your creative process. Repeat as needed for your second-lowest score.

    If your *lowest* season was:

Spring: You may need more inspiration, innovation, and "spark" in your creative practice. Focus especially on the Spring activities in this book and try something new. Julia Cameron's "artist's dates" would probably be productive for you.[11] Most important, break a few rules (including your own). A great way to start is to complete a Spring activity, such as Break a Rule or Conspire with Clouds, no matter what time of year you're in now. Finally, if you're weak in spring energy, it may be because you—like many in our overworked culture—are stuck in summer's drive for productivity or grinding through winter's to-do list to survive. If so, set aside more wintery time to rest and regenerate. It will help ready you for a spring burst.

Summer: You're missing some playful energy and abundance, and your productivity may be suffering as a result. Or perhaps you're too focused on making every moment, every brush stroke, every work session count, and not enough on explorations that can bear fruit in the future. Schedule time for a creative intensive—fast drafting or a weekend or weeklong retreat to do little more than create. Find the artsy child inside and let her out for some fun—such as by embarking on a project you promise to never show anyone else. (You can always decide later to change your mind about sharing it.) Focus on the Summer activities in this book, such as Shed Your Shoes, Find a Familiar, and Let Your Body Inspire You. Get back into your body and senses, and use those physical sensations to inform work that will be better for it.

Autumn: You're probably good at getting started and making progress, but maybe not so great at polishing and finishing, right? Or maybe you resist sharing your work with others. Either way, you need to let go of something—a fear, a habit of overscheduling yourself, that project that's ready to meet the world, or maybe the shiny new ideas that always pop up to distract you before you're really done with the last one. Do a little introspection with the Autumn activities in this book, especially Catch Reflections and Release What's No Longer Useful, and consider doing others with a creative friend. Teaming up with someone else can make it more fun and help you hold yourself more accountable for bringing results to fruition.

Winter: You might be avoiding the sheer endurance work of getting through the hard parts, whether for you that means obtaining and incorporating feedback, working through blocks, or perhaps marketing your work. The solution might be more "butt in chair" time, but the reverse may also be true: The odds are good that you're not giving yourself enough time to simply rest, regenerate, and let your subconscious work on those blocks—which are often a sign of either exhaustion or resistance to plumbing emotional depths. Lean on your creative community for support. Try a class or other educational activity as a lower-energy way to plant seeds for the future. Be sure to give such seeds the rest that nature often requires for germination (known as cold stratification) by spending some relaxed time with introspective Winter activities, such as Take Stock with a Snowflake, Rest with the Rain, and Gnaw Your Creative Bone.

If you'd like to learn what's behind the recommendations above, keep reading. Chapter 3 explores the unique energies of each season and how they resonate with us psychologically and culturally. It helps clarify why the activities to follow are assigned to one season or another. Chapters 4 and 5 provide practical guidance for getting the most out of this book.

But don't hesitate to skip ahead to a season and try an activity that appeals. Unless you're a mathematician or quantum physicist, creativity is a practice, not an intellectual task. Like the seasons themselves, it's experiential, and how a creative impulse feels—and what you do with it—is more important than what you *know* about it. Creativity is all about action.

So go play, if you like. You can always come back for the explanations during a lull on a drab winter's day.

More than a cycle: The spiral of life

The seasons and your creative journey are not cycles that strictly repeat. Rather, they advance through time in a spiral. This ancient symbol of life and time, seen everywhere from the fiddleheads of a fern to the arms of our Milky Way galaxy, reminds us that who we are this spring is different from who we were last spring simply for having lived through the year.

Similarly, every creative idea or project, even every failed experiment, is another turn through the spiral that moves your craft forward. It may feel at times like you're going in circles and covering old ground, but the accumulating seasons of your creative life continue to drive your skills and work forward. That's why you can keep using this book over time, revisiting an activity you've done before. You'll be a changed person the second time through, and perhaps working on a different creative project. The activity may resonate differently or be newly productive each time. Comparing your experiences from one cycle to the next can uncover themes or challenges worth more exploration—or help you recognize your own growth, quietly accumulating like the chambers of a nautilus shell.

Every creative project is another turn through the spiral that moves your craft forward.

© iStock.com/Carlos Sanchez

Chapter 3:
Exploring the Energies of Each Season

The energies of each season and how they influence us—our psychological, emotional, and cultural associations—are based originally in close observation of nature. In addition to being creative, humans had to be shameless voyeurs to survive.

If we watch anything more closely than nature, however, it's ourselves. As a result, we've drawn parallels between the seasons and our own lives and behavior. These connections are found everywhere from traditional Chinese and Ayurvedic medicine to Greek and Celtic cosmology, Egyptian alchemy, and the Medicine Wheel concept sacred to Ojibwe and other Plains Native Americans. While every culture adds its own spin, the influences associated with each season are relatively consistent because they start from a common foundation of biology, ecology, and sociology.

In addition to associating young children with the new life of spring and white-haired elders with winter, we ascribe related psychological states and personality traits to each season. For instance, innocence, curiosity, and playfulness seem to belong to the early parts of our lives and the year, while self-sufficiency, responsibility, and self-sacrifice describe both the adults who sustain their communities and the frigid part of the year where those traits matter most for our shared survival. See the table that follows for a few more examples.

The influences associated with each season are relatively consistent.

Common seasonal associations

	Spring	Summer	Autumn	Winter
Biology	Birth	Growth	Maturation	Death
Ecology	Fertility	Growth	Reproduction & decay	Rest & regeneration
Human development	Infancy	Childhood	Adolescence, early adulthood	Later adulthood, old age
Developmental task	Awakening	Exploration	Introspection, relation	Reproduction, community
Role in society	Dependence	Individuation	Independence	Leadership, legacy
Personal qualities	Innocence, curiosity, rebellion	Playful exuberance, adventurousness	Sensuality, self-consciousness	Generosity, work ethic, self-sacrifice

From the obvious to the intuitive

Because humans are good at abstract thought and driven to create meaning and order in our lives, various thinkers have gone further to organize other aspects of our experience into this seasonal matrix. The results are based more on intuition than on any "-ology," but they resonate with many people.

For instance, the multiple dimensions of being human—spiritual, physical, emotional, and intellectual—fit neatly into the cycle, in that order. There's no question that all four dimensions are with us our entire lives, but once you've decided that adolescence goes with autumn and adulthood with winter, for instance, it's easy to concede (or at least imagine) that emotional energy rules the former and rational thought ascends in the latter.

The sensations we perceive from the world can be sorted similarly, even though we have five primary senses, not four. We say, "spring is in the air" when birdsong and cherry blossoms engage the senses brought to us on the breeze—hearing and scent—after a long, stifling winter indoors. Summer's focus on visible, physical growth and therefore the body places the most full-body sense, touch, firmly in those warmest months. Harvest feasts emphasize taste as well as feelings like gratitude and nostalgia. As Jane Austen noted in *Persuasion*, "[A]utumn—that season of peculiar and inexhaustible influence on the mind of taste and tenderness..." Meanwhile, winter draws our attention to vision, both for what we can no longer see in the dark and for the interior or shared visions of art, storytelling, and dreams.

A host of other mental and emotional connections accompany each season, too. For instance, spring's increasing light and emergent plant life make it reasonable to associate new ideas, discoveries, and change with this season, along with related feelings, such as awe, excitement, and the confusion that may come with change. Or consider the generosity and community goodwill that characterize the dark holidays around winter solstice. With almost magnetic force, each season evokes individual and communal responses that have helped us survive over generations. The full range of seasonal energies, as they apply specifically to creativity, are explored in greater depth in the introduction to each season later in this book.

Secondary seasonal associations

	Spring	Summer	Autumn	Winter
Human dimension	Spirit	Body	Emotion/Psyche	Mind
Sensory experience	Scent, hearing	Touch	Taste	Vision
Concepts	Inspiration, discovery, mobility, change	Exploration, development, success	Completion, collaboration, celebration	Mutual support, stability, persistence
Emotions	Curiosity, awe, excitement, confusion	Passion, joy, courage, anger	Empathy, gratitude, sadness, grief	Hope, fear, determination, endurance

Do such extrapolations push too far into fancy? Probably—although as noted, research supports a seasonal effect on personality and mental health that roughly aligns with these concepts. But if these seasonal associations didn't resonate, we wouldn't nod our heads to this quote from artist Yoko Ono:

> *"Spring passes and one remembers one's innocence.*
> *Summer passes and one remembers one's exuberance.*
> *Autumn passes and one remembers one's reverence.*
> *Winter passes and one remembers one's perseverance."*

Ultimately, despite ongoing neurological study, creativity is more art than science. It draws heavily on image, sensory experience, and metaphor, all of which fuel the associations above. And when you want to encourage your imagination, few things work better than other imaginative leaps to spark fresh ways of thinking. Scientific or not, the influences we associate with each season can inspire and motivate you.

Fire, water, spikes, and wings

But wait, there's more! Take a look back at your Creative Critter Shopping Spree. There's a method to the madness of those choices.

A variety of philosophical traditions, from the ancient Greeks and Ayurveda practitioners to modern poets and business consultants,[12] view the natural world—including human temperaments—through a lens of four or five basic elements: air, fire, water, and earth, with the frequent addition of ether or space. (Traditional Chinese medicine tracks this somewhat differently, using earth, water, and fire, plus wood and metal.) Earth's seasons also have been linked with those four (or sometimes five) basic elements. The four cardinal directions—east, south, west, and north—are sometimes included too, most notably in the Ojibwe medicine wheel. Such representations bring together multiple natural cycles and cosmologies to

The influences we associate with each season can inspire and motivate you.

illuminate human experience and our relationships with the Earth and each other.

Each element, like each season, is broadly associated with physical, mental, psychological, and behavioral traits and is arranged on a spectrum from air (light and diffuse) to earth (heavy and dense). For instance, air is linked with our intangible intellects and thoughts that can shift unexpectedly, like the wind, bringing insight or driving erratic behavior. Fire suggests passion, courage, anger, and transformation of the sort that could be destructive or might produce warmth and light. Water, whose depths are strongly associated with emotion, introspection, and the psyche, can bring life through bubbly cheer or drown us in "sinking" feelings of sadness. Earth evokes fertility, nurturing, practicality, and stability, which could mean rigid or stubborn. As you might guess from these examples, each element represents strengths and potential weaknesses.

These four earthly elements also align pretty intuitively with the seasons and their cycle of birth, growth, maturity, and decline. Specifically:

> *The four earthly elements also align with the seasons.*

Air and fire combine in spring. The season brings a sense of lightness or freedom after winter's darkness, thick clothing, and heavy snow. This lightness is reflected in the insubstantial, hard-to-grasp elements of air and fire. Think newly warm breezes and Latin's *inspirare*, which means "breathe into" and is the source for our word inspiration. Also consider figures of speech such as "the winds of change." The breeze also brings us sounds and aromas, the senses most closely linked with this season, along with birds, butterflies, kites, and other common symbols of spring. Add the fire of the returning sun, the spark of new ideas, which are whipped into flame with the right gust of air, and the transformative power of flames, all appropriate in the season more closely associated with change than any other. The highly mobile and unpredictable aspects of both air and fire also reverberate, given spring's connection with impulsivity, the restlessness and frequent foolishness of spring fever, our intangible spirits, and emotions that feel fluttery and "ungrounded," such as anxiety, confusion, sexual awakening, and romantic crushes.

Fire and earth meet in summer. In this season, we can't help noticing the fire of midday heat and light, as well as the blaze of growth they summon from the earth. Many people, activating their physical bodies, garden, camp, hike, play, and interact with the earth itself more intensely in summer than at other times. Burning sunsets cap long days, which give us time to push past physical and metaphorical limits and explore. Campfires, barbecue flames, and fireworks all express the exuberance of the season (and wildfires increasingly represent summer energies out of control).

Earth and water work together in autumn. The earth's harvest grows juicy and ripens before encroaching twilights and increasing rain collude in fall's decay. In some regions, monsoons blur the transition between summer and fall, and these dramatic rains may be singled out as a season in its own right. But most of the Northern Hemisphere transitions more gradually from earth's pumpkins, golden leaves, compost piles, and stocked woodsheds to mud puddles, fog, and chill morning dews. The world sinks into a darkness that prompts turning within, literally to our homes to taste harvest's fruits and metaphorically to the watery depths of emotions.

Water and air rule winter. In fact, the word "winter" comes originally from root words that mean either wet or wind. Both seem to apply, since this flintiest of seasons surrounds us with water that arrives on harsh winds and may be condensed into snow and ice, as if the loss of the sun has solidified both the water and the air. The two come together most dramatically on looming mountain peaks and at Santa's North Pole, whose most famous resident travels through the air. Elsewhere, the Earth shrinks back to essential rocks and bare soil. Constrained by short, dark days, we focus on the airy intellectual life through education, stories, and dreams of the future. Finally, the Judeo-Christian story of creation is not the only one that begins with a divine wind or breath moving over the deep, dark potential of water. Such are the conditions prior to life exploding in spring.

These elemental alignments inform some of the activities in this book, including the Creative Critter options. Fins and slime were autumn choices, for instance, thanks to that season's link to water and everything it represents. And since images are the primary language of the subconscious, an affinity for those choices suggests that, on some level, autumn images and energies resonate most strongly for the artist who selects them.

Winter
Midnight
Old Age/Death
Rest
Renewal

Water, Air
Legacy
Responsibility
Mind/Intellect
Vision

Spring
Dawn
Birth & Rebirth
Innocence
Inspiration

Air, Fire
Inception
Change
Spirit, Symbol
Hearing, Scent

Autumn
Earth, Water
Maturity
Introspection
Emotions/Psyche
Taste

Sunset
Maturity
Ripening
Harvest

Summer
Fire, Earth
Growth
Stability
Physical Body
Touch

Noon
Youth
Blooming
Development

Your mileage may vary

Of course, depending on your local climate and life experiences, your personal associations with a season might be different from any or all of those listed here. The activities in this guide draw on them because they map so neatly to aspects of the creative process, but they're neither universal nor absolute.

Most particularly, various traditions see the alignment between the seasons and the elements differently because they're rooted in different climate and cultural terrain. Some systems link the earth element to winter, for instance. Rather than associating earth with summer's plant growth or autumn's ripening fruit, these alternate systems justifiably pair winter's harsh cold and darkness with barren rocks or caves, the parts of earth that become prominent when the other seasons have passed. Plus there's something satisfying about a linear progression from the lightest element, air, in the spring to the densest, earth, in the winter.

In fact, different aspects of earth can be mapped to every season, including spring's freshly thawed soil for planting and autumn's lush harvest and decaying vegetation. After all, without the planet and its motion, we wouldn't have seasons—or be here at all. This example shows how condensing all physical existence and human experience to four or five elemental building blocks, and then assigning them to the seasons, is almost laughably reductive. Like any oversimplification, these ideas have their limits.

The seasonal map can help us navigate a difficult creative landscape.

But even an imperfect map can provide inspiration for where we might go and guide us on how to get there. Similarly, the seasonal map can help us navigate a difficult creative landscape. It needs only to prompt introspection, activate our imaginations, and nudge us into actual motion. The seasonal activities that follow do that.

Speaking of journeys: archetypes

For creatives, especially those who tell stories, it can be productive to add one more dimension to our seasonal map.

Recall the hero's journey, whose structure echoes the seasons. In addition to the hero, the journey is peopled with familiar character types, such as the trusty sidekick, the wise mentor, or the ruler who may not be so wise. These characters are also archetypes, and the hero's journey is frequently seen as a model of human development in which the hero begins as an archetypal Innocent, grows through the trials they face, defeats death or their own shadow in the form of a villain or monster, and returns home to acclaim as the Hero, often becoming a Ruler in the process. Although we're each the hero of our own story, we also play archetypal roles in the stories of others. We may be caretakers, mentors, sidekicks, or villains, for instance.

Mythologists and psychologists recognize many character archetypes, but about a dozen stand out as the most common. (The minor variations from one scholar's list to the next aren't important for our purposes.) They're often arranged on a wheel—because, like the hero's journey itself, the most frequently cited character archetypes also reflect the cycle of seasons and can be grouped according to their seasonal affinities and traits.

Spring: Innocent, Messenger, Trickster, Rebel. The Innocent archetype, which the hero usually embodies to start, lives in the new life of spring as expressed through baby animals, tender buds, and fragile new shoots. The Messenger archetype, although not always included in the most basic dozen, helps kick off the action by inviting the hero to the adventure, as R2-D2 does for Luke Skywalker in *Star Wars Episode IV: A New Hope*. The Messenger's connection to spring goes further, however. It's also manifest in Hermes and Mercury, the Greek and Roman expressions of this archetype. As gods of fertility, they bring new life and launch the agricultural year.

The Messenger is sometimes conflated or combined with the Trickster, who's found in the season's unpredictable weather and seemingly dead branches that burst into leaf. This Trickster may be unreliable, disguised, or both. Like the Messenger, a Trickster often kicks off a story, but the Trickster is more likely to reappear later. Think of the wolf in Little Red Riding Hood, MacBeth's witches, or Puck in *A Midsummer Night's Dream*. Finally, the Rebel, the embodiment of spring's fresh ideas, might upend convention by embarking on an unexpected or forbidden hero's journey like Joan of Arc did or, conversely, resist the call to adventure until it won't be denied.

Summer: Explorer, Lover, Caretaker. During summer and the Innocent's (or Rebel's) early adventures and trials, they become an Explorer, taking risks, losing their naiveté, and pushing toward the unknown. In this phase of the journey and year, a Lover—the result of spring's fertility urges—may supply the heat of passion to motivate or support the hero, or possibly become a distracting temptation. Lady Macbeth manages to fill both roles in her husband's tragedy. Meanwhile, the Caregiver archetype, who often appears as a trusted sidekick in the vein of Sam Gamgee, accompanies the hero forward. Like a gardener who encourages summertime's growth, the caregiver provides stability after the change and possible rebellion of spring.

Autumn: Shadow, Warrior, Magician. Come autumn, the adventurer approaches their ultimate challenge, whether in the form of a monster, looming death, or their own encroaching Shadow. Disappointment, failure, or a sense of betrayal (prompted by the departing sun) frequently initiate the ultimate battle, converting the adventurer into a figurative or literal Warrior. They may fight with help from—or as—the Magician, who traffics in the invisible as summer's light fades and who straddles the boundary between life and death as Gandalf and Yoda both do.

Winter: Hero, Ruler, Artist, Sage. If the story is not a tragedy, the hero endures every challenge and battle, eventually returning home in a new role, as the capital-H Hero. They may become their community's Ruler, sharing their treasure as a king might oversee equitable distribution of the dwindling remains of fall's harvest. Despite winter's persistent threat of death, the Ruler strives to protect the community while the Sage and Artist record and recount their great deeds, prompting all to consider our own legacies and inspiring others to begin new quests come spring. For instance, Bilbo Baggins is one Hero who returns home not to rule (that's Aragorn's role) but to record his own adventures and inspire the next generation, namely Frodo.

As with the four elements, this seasonal alignment of key archetypes is intended mostly to provoke thought. Part of the power of archetypes is their flexibility, so I'll be the first to cheer if you want to insist that, for instance, the Artist archetype belongs in the spring with new ideas—or shouldn't be limited to any one season. If so, this section will have served its purpose simply by nudging you to your own conclusions. But I hope it will also inspire creative responses in the later activities that draw on it.

Inspiration is all about new connections.

A map for navigating your own creative journey

When the elements and character archetypes are included, we're left with a detailed matrix (see the page after next) that incorporates the range of seasonal associations. Just as a topographical map offers a different perspective from the one used by the directional app on your phone, this seasonal map provides a fresh perspective from which to view your artistic process. Using it to explore the territory of your own creativity can prompt new connections and insights or suggest new approaches to your work habits and projects. That's why it's useful: creativity demands exploration and experimentation, and inspiration is all about new connections.

But whether this perspective resonates for you or not, the time you spend in nature working with this book is almost certain to have practical, positive effects on your creativity. The research is clear that time immersed in a natural setting clarifies our thinking, calms our nerves, improves our physical and mental health, instills a sense of connectedness, and boosts creativity, creative reasoning, and inspiration.[13] These effects can only benefit your creative work.

	Spring	Summer	Autumn	Winter
Biology	Birth	Growth	Maturation	Death
Ecology	Fertility	Growth	Reproduction & decay	Rest & regeneration
Human development	Infancy	Childhood	Adolescence, early adulthood	Later adulthood, old age
Developmental task	Awakening	Exploration	Introspection, relation	Reproduction, community
Role in society	Dependence	Individuation	Independence	Leadership, legacy
Personal qualities	Innocence, curiosity, rebellion	Playful exuberance, adventurousness	Sensuality, self-consciousness	Generosity, work ethic, self-sacrifice
Human dimension	Spirit	Body	Emotion/Psyche	Mind
Sensory experience	Scent, hearing	Touch	Taste	Vision
Concepts	Inspiration, discovery, mobility, change	Exploration, development, success	Completion, collaboration, celebration	Mutual support, stability, persistence
Emotions	Curiosity, awe, excitement, confusion	Passion, joy, courage, anger	Empathy, gratitude, sadness, grief	Hope, fear, determination, endurance
Element	Air, fire	Fire, earth	Earth, water	Water, air
Character archetype	Innocent, Messenger, Trickster, Rebel	Explorer, Lover, Caretaker	Warrior, Magician, Shadow	Hero, Ruler, Artist, Sage

Chapter 4:
Whose Season Is It, Anyway?

Wait. If we're going to address creativity season by season, what counts as spring? When does summer start? Although the seasons themselves transcend cultures, when one season ends and the next begins depends on who you ask and where they live.

First, the tilt of the Earth means that the Northern Hemisphere's summer is the Southern Hemisphere's winter, and vice versa. Stuck in between, people who live near the equator experience relatively little variation in temperature or daylight over the year.

But it gets worse. If you try to plot them on a calendar, the seasons get complicated even in one hemisphere. When asked to name the "official" first day of spring, astronomers give one answer and weather forecasters another, not to mention academic calendars, liturgical calendars, and traditional calendars, such as those developed by the Celts and the Chinese, which are based on both sun and moon—

Screech, clatter…crash! Stop. Forget official answers. All these systems, even traditional lunisolar calendars, are intellectual constructs, jimmied to divide evenly despite a planetary orbit that's elliptical, not round, and a solar year that's an awkward 365 days and 348.8 minutes. For this book, such constructs don't matter, because my aim is to better connect you with how seasons stimulate your own mind and body.

When you completed the Seasonal Tendencies questionnaire, you identified the season of your birth instinctively,

> *My aim is to better connect you with how seasons stimulate your own mind and body.*

based on your own ideas of when each season begins or ends. Not only that, but you know from experience that wherever you live, the local climate can vary. One summer may effectively end in late August. Another year it seems to stretch into October. Take each season as you feel it wherever you live, regardless of the calendar date.

Why flexibility is important

Here's why I think such flexibility is important: I have a problem with March.

Although I loved school, my distrust of its dogma started early. My third-grade classroom included a bulletin board decorated each month with what passed in the 1960s for memes. November featured a turkey, of course. Hearts floated through February. But March's board offered nothing but lies.

First, it shouted "Spring!" along with the old chestnut, "In like a lion, out like a lamb." Where I lived, the weather did not comply. March in the Pacific Northwest neither roars like a lion nor softens to a cuddly lamb. It's more like a concrete cell whose roof leaks. Any chance of snow has passed and the showers supposedly not due until April have splattered continuously since November.

But that wasn't our bulletin board's only mistake. The image for the month was a kite. Excited, I assembled a traditional paper diamond nearly as tall as my little brother. My dad, who worked for the Air Force and knew about flight, gave me a stick wrapped with enough string to snag the military planes that roared over our house. But they were never in danger, because I discovered you can't fly a kite in a downpour. Not in a sprinkle, drizzle, mizzle, or mist, either. The wind I was promised for March never blew.

Spring weather does come to the Northwest eventually. Later, I would fly my green kite so high that reeling it back in took the better part of an hour. But only on breezy summer or fall days, and I never forgave March for the disappointment.

Take each season as you feel it, wherever you live.

Subsequent March events, including the sudden death of a loved one, affirmed the truth—in my world, March is winter's last dirty trick. I skip it when I can, leaving home for somewhere with blue skies and breezes.

Consider this permission

So take my permission to discard "official" seasonal definitions you may have learned. Pay more attention to what's going on both inside your body and outside your home. If you live in a tropical climate and January's new beginnings feel like spring to you, great. (Just don't skip winter altogether. It serves an important purpose, both for nature and for our psyches.) You get to decide based on the natural world that surrounds you and your personal associations with various times of the year.

Identifying your own seasons is important even if you don't hold grudges against certain months. A math teacher, a wheat farmer, and a snowplow driver most likely feel differently about summer and winter. Their busiest workloads, free times, and attitudes about sun, rain, or snow all play roles. Their associations also may be influenced by factors ranging from personality traits to whether their families include kids. The activities for each season in this book allow space for such personal associations and quirks. If you like, clarify those personal associations with the questions on the next page.

If you're the sort of person who tends to follow rules and needs structure—and I haven't convinced you to cut loose with spring fever and break a small rule by jumping ahead—I've got you. Maybe you're procrastinating, but that's okay, too. There's another word for procrastination—preparation. It's an impulse of winter. The influence of such wintertime energy, when not overdone, can be highly productive. If your heart longs for a bit more preparation, complete the activity on the next page and read on for a few tips on using this book. Otherwise, flip ahead to whatever season you're in, or to a season whose energy you need to explore, and dive in to an activity now.

If your heart longs for a bit more preparation, read on. Otherwise, flip ahead and dive in.

Define Your Own Seasons

How this can help you: Gain insight into personal associations with each season to better harness their energies and more effectively use this book.

1. **Answer the following questions**, perhaps using a journal to explore them:
    - What feels like the start of summer for you? *For example, June 1, school vacation, or whenever the thermometer hits 70 or 80?*
    - What heralds fall? Back-to-school energy has been programmed into most of us, but your triggers might be football, the first fallen leaf, frost, or something else altogether.
    - When do you know winter's here?
    - What do you consider the first sign of spring?
    - If you secretly feel cheated of any of these four seasons based on your local climate, what's missing? What aspects of it do you long for most, and why?
    - What feels like the most restful time of the year to you, and why? Consider treating this time as your winter for the activities in this book.
    - Does your life have a fifth season—a period of at least two weeks—recognized by your culture or workplace or that you otherwise need to carve out in addition to the usual four? How does that personal season affect your creativity? *For instance, the year-end holiday season can feel like a time unto itself when normal rules don't apply (and creative work can be difficult). A sport season might be another example.*
    - If you got to invent your own fifth or sixth season, when would it happen, how long would it last, and what would you call it? *For instance, I love the first few weeks of January, after the hectic holidays and while the year still echoes with the unknown ahead. I usually get a lot of creative work done in this season, which I call Possibility. Then I become sick of darkness and damp, and my winter hits.*
2. **Remember or refer to your answers as you try the activities** in the sections to follow. They'll resonate more when aligned with your own internal seasons.
3. *Storytellers*: **Answer the questions above for a protagonist or antagonist** to deepen their characterizations and set up conflicts with people around them, who may operate on different implicit schedules.

Chapter 5:
How to Use This Workbook from Here

▶ **Start where you are**

We experience seasons as a cycle. Books, however, are linear, and this one had to start somewhere. But once you've reached this point, it's not intended to be read front to back. Instead, turn to the section that best aligns with the season you're living through now. (Or, if you're starting near the end of a season, perhaps with the season that will soon begin.)

As an alternative, take advantage of the seasonal archetype by focusing on creativity over a single day. Choose a Spring activity in the morning, a Summer activity at midday, an Autumn activity in late afternoon or evening, and a Winter activity just before bedtime.

Finally, check in with your own emotions and life situation. Maybe you've just begun some new role or life phase that makes spring energies attractive. If so, try a few Spring activities no matter the time of year. Similarly, if you've been through a difficult period, you may find yourself weary and longing mostly for sleep, self-care, or turning within to your own thoughts. In modern life, most of us get too little rest—too little of what's naturally offered by winter's long nights. But you can nurture yourself anytime with a few of the Winter activities. This is the concept behind "wintering," regardless of what season nature displays. And being aware of your own impulses and their resonance—or dissonance—with nature is the first step to better alignment with it.

> *Nurture yourself anytime with a few of the Winter activities.*

Ultimately, the idea is to draw on the energies and priorities of the natural world to amplify the creative powers of your own internal landscape. When your inner energies match those outside, they'll resonate more deeply, which makes them easier to recognize and put to work. Then you can surf the wave instead of being bowled over by it.

▶ Define nature broadly

Time with nature doesn't require wilderness or hardship. Gardening is one way many creative people turn to nature, even in cities. Parks, riverwalks, shorelines, backyards, and houseplants are others. The most urban of cities have cloudscapes, if you'll only look up. Or look down—there are exercises in this book you can complete simply by finding a patch of bare ground to watch ants, or earthworms rising to rain, or a sprout pushing up through a crack. Stop at a tree surrounded by sidewalk to spy a shy bird or inspect a caterpillar nest. In large part, reconnecting with nature is about slowing down to the pace of the sun and the seasons, sharpening our awareness, and paying attention. Reconnecting with creativity similarly requires pausing to notice both external and internal tides. Ultimately, nature can serve as a mirror for our own hearts and subconscious minds.

Reconnecting with nature—and creativity—is about slowing down and paying attention.

▶ Embrace constraints

Researchers and many creative people acknowledge that, perhaps counterintuitively, constraints foster creativity. Examples of useful constraints range from external deadlines, which help light a fire under so many creatives, to the structures of specific poetic forms, to challenges such as trying to write a novel without using the letter E. Somehow, such fences summon a more playful spirit and point the way toward new ways to dance around the constraint.

This book uses the structure imposed by the cycle of seasons as exactly that kind of useful constraint. If you like, you can take this idea even further. For instance, if I suggest an activity that's not feasible for you (such as walking outdoors), find a small window on nature that is. Study a house spider for 10 minutes, for instance—or slice an apple and examine it, with all of your senses, more intimately than you have before. Such focus can invite your imagination to play and open new perspectives.

Similarly, instead of collecting leaves, stones, and sticks for an activity, try it with spices or supplies from your refrigerator. See what happens if you use only half the time I suggest. Or use only one hand. Or do it with your eyes closed. For most activities, it's not the result that matters. It's the energy or insights the process stirs up and how they can help you create beauty and meaning on the way to a deeper connection with yourself and your world. As poet Mary Oliver noted, you're opening the door to "a silence in which another voice may speak."

> *For most activities, it's not the result that matters. It's the energy or insights the process stirs up.*

> *It doesn't have to be*
> *the blue iris, it could be*
> *weeds in a vacant lot, or a few*
> *small stones; just*
> *pay attention, then patch*
> *a few words together and don't try*
> *to make them elaborate, this isn't*
> *a contest but the doorway*
> *into thanks, and a silence in which*
> *another voice may speak.*

— "Praying" by Mary Oliver (*Thirst*, Beacon Press, 2006)

▶ Be curious and willing to stretch

The activities that follow vary from quick to involved, and the more challenging activities are noted. In general, the easiest and quickest activities for each season are presented first.

It can be useful to bounce between them, oscillating between snacks and full meals, rather than saving all the more complex suggestions for last. You could also spread a single activity, particularly one with journaling questions, over a whole week. Regardless, the more attention and energy you put into even an easy one, the more you're likely to get from it.

Remember that growth can be uncomfortable. If you find yourself resisting an activity or journaling prompt, get curious about why. Resistance is often a clue to submerged feelings worth exploring. It's the fears and emotions we don't want to acknowledge that typically hold us back, both creatively and in other parts of our lives. As Jung noted, what we resist rarely goes away; it festers. Acknowledging resistance and dealing with whatever prompts it can help us to break through the blocks to greater achievement. When you notice resistance, try that activity with a creative friend to support you, cheer you on, compare results, and maybe talk about the emotions that surface. Or if necessary, come back to the point of resistance some other time.

Finally, if you're a storyteller, many of the activities can be done from two different perspectives. The first is personal, revealing your own attitudes toward your creative life or a specific project. The second is from the viewpoints of your current main character, antagonist, or both. Working through an activity as your character can provide insight into their personalities or motivations to help you solve story challenges. Try both approaches over time.

> *If you're a storyteller, working through an activity as your character can provide insight.*

▶ Draw on the power of ritual

A large body of research indicates that rituals can boost our moods and increase both confidence and self-discipline, which in turn measurably improve performance.[14] Rituals also alert ourselves and others to significant change. They interrupt our daily lives to say, "Hey! This is important." Whether it's throwing away the last half-pack of cigarettes or a wild bachelorette party before becoming a wife, these signals are noted by our subconscious minds, where they make it easier to move forward into the new reality they mark.

That's why many activities in this book encourage rituals. But rituals are particularly appropriate for creatives because both art and rituals transmute symbolic meaning into the material world, and convert the material world into symbols. Examples from ritual range from the wafers of Holy Communion to birthday candles. Writers and artists do exactly the same, extracting ideas and metaphors from physical human experiences and then making those ideas tangible in their work, whether books, paintings, or dance moves.

Such transmutation is an invaluable skill for artists. This book offers you practice by encouraging you to view the natural world through a symbolic lens and assign psychological meanings to material things—or vice versa.

But you can't get the full benefits of a ritual you only read or imagine. So please try at least a few of the rituals suggested here for each season. Any twinge of discomfort or self-consciousness is part what makes ritual a powerful tool. Besides, if a ritual makes you squirm, remember that creative people are frequently seen as eccentric. In fact, there's evidence that eccentricity and creativity go together.[15] So the more eccentric you feel, perhaps the more creative you are!

Still, that self-consciousness is a good reason to perform rituals with creative friends. You can laugh together about feeling silly while fully marking the moment, increasing your accountability for the change, and sharing the benefits of ritual with them.

In particular, if you want to maximize how much this book helps you, start with the small ritual that follows.

Rituals can measurably improve performance.

Set a Clear Goal Now

How this can help you: Writing down and sharing your goals and how you'll handle obstacles will help ensure this book feeds your creativity, not just your bookshelf.

My goal or goals for this book:
(One is enough! But there's room in the woods for overachievers.)

1.

2.

3.

The obstacles that might stop me from achieving these goals:

1.

2.

3.

My strategies for overcoming those obstacles:

1.

2.

3.

I'm sharing these goals with (*who?*) _____

by (*how?*) _____

When? Right now! Or, if not, by _____

Congratulations! With this activity and the others you've already completed, you're putting down roots to support creative growth.

▶ Set a clear goal now

Research shows that we're more likely to achieve goals when we write them down, share them with others, and develop strategies for overcoming the most likely hurdles.[16]

Nature recognizes this truth, after a fashion. A pine nut doesn't simply start growing and wait to see whether it becomes an evergreen tree, a pineapple, or the bird known as a pine siskin. Through genetics, it *plans* to become a pine tree, and it starts with strategies that give it the best chance—such as waiting to sprout until frozen soil thaws and sending out nimble roots that can curl around stones.

You're at least as clever as a pine nut, right? So consider what you hope to accomplish and write those goals on the page at left or in your journal. A few realistic examples:

- Have fun creating only for yourself.
- Establish a more intentional creative practice.
- Explore new impulses or directions.
- Rediscover the joy of creativity (which sometimes fades under challenges or disappointments).
- Gain ideas to share with your creative community.

Don't stop with the goal itself. Like the pine nut, acknowledge in advance what might get in the way and develop a strategy for clearing those hurdles. Some of the barriers or habits that could hinder your success include:

- Feeling like you don't have time for the activities.
- Reading the activities without trying them. (As with muscles, you can't strengthen your creativity merely by thinking about it.)
- Negative self-talk about your creativity.
- A false belief that every spare moment should be directed toward existing projects (whether that means your novel or your half-remodeled basement).

Research shows we're more likely to achieve goals when we write them down and share them with others.

When you recognize barriers in advance, you can develop a strategy to overcome them. For instance, to beat the sample challenges listed above:

- Set aside a regular time on your calendar—say an hour a week—for an activity in this book. Also identify what *won't* happen then. (One less hour of social media, for instance, or a household chore that can be skipped now and then.) Or, if you keep a journal, flip ahead and write "Do a *Wildly Inspired* activity" several times as prompts when you reach those pages.
- Find a creative friend who will do activities with you—or at least serve as an accountability buddy by regularly asking about and celebrating your progress.
- Create a mantra to help silence your inner critic. Try, "Every sunrise is a new chance to create well."
- Remember that just as physical labor can be more productive when we take time for sleep, creative labor benefits from time off. (Besides, many activities in this book can be completed with a specific project in mind and may help you remove a block, solve a problem, or generate momentum.)

Share your goals with someone—email them to a friend, post them on social media or your refrigerator, or read them aloud to your dog.

Last but not least, decide what season you're in (or about to enter)—or which season might help you find more creative balance. Turn to that part of this book, choose an activity, and get started!

Acknowledge in advance what might get in the way and develop a strategy for clearing those hurdles.

Part 1 Endnotes

1—In my view, the territory of the *anima mundi* overlaps with or is part of what Islamic philosopher Henry Corbin called the *Mundus Imaginalis*, the imaginal world—which is not imaginary in the Western sense but quite real and related to the concept of Platonic ideals. Its subtle energies infuse and animate the world of matter and nature the way the life force animates us. If you're interested in learning more, I suggest Christian mystic Cynthia Bourgeault's quick blog series on the topic starting at https://www.cynthiabourgeault.org/blog/2018/11/13/introducing-the-imaginal

2—Vartanian, Oshin et al. "The Creative Brain Under Stress: Considerations for Performance in Extreme Environments." *Frontiers in Psychology* Vol. 11: 2020. https://doi.org/10.3389/fpsyg.2020.585969

3—For a clear explanation of objective correlative and an example, read "What Is the Objective Correlative?" by author Ingrid Sundberg on her blog at https://ingridsnotes.wordpress.com/2013/05/14/what-is-the-objective-correlative/

4—Bachelard, Gaston. *The Poetics of Space* (1957). Maria Jolas, trans. New York: Penguin Classics (2014)

5—There's evidence that our inclination to be larks or owls is set when we're born. People born between 4 p.m. and midnight are more likely to be night owls, while people born between midnight and 6 a.m. are usually larks. (Those born between 6 a.m. and 4 p.m. can probably blame family or social conditioning, since there's no solid relationship for them. Of course, society encourages larks.) Do you fit the pattern?

The seasons influence us similarly—at least at the statistical level. More than one study has shown that people born in February and March are more likely to be highly successful visual or performing artists, while successful writers are more likely to be born in May or June. Other times of the year favor newborn scientists, mathematicians, and medical professionals. But if you don't align with tendency, don't fret! As with most things, effort can make up the difference.

Furthermore, multiple studies have found that in the Northern Hemisphere, people born in spring (especially April and May) have the highest risk of dying from heart-related conditions. People born in late fall (especially November and December) have the lowest. Other studies also note that those born in September seem to be at higher risk of death from infections.

I'm not trying to scare April, May, or fall babies. The risk factors involved aren't very big, especially compared with how you live your life. But it's interesting evidence of how we're affected by seasons in ways we may not be aware of, that persist our whole lives, and that even experts can't explain. (They suspect it's related to vitamin D in the womb, though.) That's a good reminder to create while we can!

My sources for this information include:

- Abeliansky, Ana Lucia, and Strulik, Holger. "Season of Birth, Health and Aging." *Economics & Human Biology* 36 (2020), pp. 100812. https://doi.org/10.1016/j.ehb.2019.100812
- Boyd, Jeffery H., et al. "Season of Birth: Schizophrenia and Bipolar Disorder." *Schizophrenia Bulletin*, 12: 2 (1986), pp. 173–186. https://doi.org/10.1093/schbul/12.2.173
- Fares, Auda. "Winter cardiovascular diseases phenomenon." *North American Journal of Medical Sciences* vol. 5,4 (2013): 266-79. https://doi.org/10.4103/1947-2714.110430
- Fuller Torrey, E., et al. "Birth Seasonality in Bipolar Disorder, Schizophrenia, Schizoaffective Disorder and Stillbirths." *Schizophrenia Research*, 21:3 (1996), pp. 141-149. https://doi.org/10.1016/0920-9964(96)00022-9
- Mazhul, Lidia A. "Seasonal Aspect of Creativity, Scientific and Artistic (Highest Levels of Achievements)." A. Fusco and R. Tomassoni (Eds.), *Psychology and Artistic Creativity*. Milano: Franco Angeli, 2017, pp. 46-56
- Marzullo, Giovanni. "Sunlight, Neurulation, and the 'Madness-Creativity' Nexus: A Schizophrenia-Like Birth-Month Effect Among Artists and Mathematicians." *Schizophrenia Research*, 117: 2–3 (2010), pp. 199-200. https://doi.org/10.1016/j.schres.2010.02.268
- Petrov, Vladimir, et al. "Measurement of Happiness—Seasonal Determination." *Measurements* 2:11 (2015), p. 92. http://metrology-bg.org/fulltextpapers/70.pdf
- Rihmer, Zoltan, et al. "Season of Birth in Bipolar Disorder," *Journal of Affective Disorders*, 294: 2021, p.116. https://doi.org/10.1016/j.jad.2021.06.083
- Sailani, M.R., et al. "Deep Longitudinal Multiomics Profiling Reveals Two Biological Seasonal Patterns in California." *Nature Communications* 11, 4933 (2020). https://doi.org/10.1038/s41467-020-18758-1
- Ueda P., et al. "Month of Birth and Cause-specific Mortality Between 50 and 80 Years: A Population-Based Longitudinal Cohort Study in Sweden." *European Journal of Epidemiology* 29:2 (Feb. 2014). pp. 89-94. https://doi.org/10.1007/s10654-014-9882-7
- Ueda P., et al. "Month of Birth and Mortality in Sweden: A Nation-Wide Population-Based Cohort Study." *PLoS ONE* 8(2): e56425 (2013). https://doi.org/10.1371/journal.pone.0056425

- Zhang, Yin, et al. "Birth Month, Birth Season, and Overall and Cardiovascular Disease Mortality in US Women: Prospective Cohort Study." *BMJ* 2019. 367:l6058. https://doi.org/10.1136/bmj.l6058
- Zoltan, Peter Erdos, et al. "Association Between Affective Temperaments and Season of Birth in a General Student Population." *Journal of Affective Disorders*, 132: 1–2 (2011), pp. 64-70. https://doi.org/10.1016/j.jad.2011.01.015

6—Norcross, John C., and Vangarelli, Dominic J. "The Resolution Solution: Longitudinal Examination of New Year's Change Attempts." Journal of Substance Abuse 1:2 (1988), pp. 1217-134. https://doi.org/10.1016/S0899-3289(88)80016-6; Moshantz de la Rocha, Hannah. "Understanding Ordinary Goal Pursuit: Describing and Predicting Success in New Year's Resolutions." Duke University, 2020. https://osf.io/preprints/thesiscommons/cdmvf_v1

7—Service, Owain, and Gallagher, Rory. *Think Small: The Surprisingly Simple Ways to Reach Big Goals*. London: Michael O'Mara Books, 2017

8—Van Gennep, Arnold. *Rites of Passage, Second Edition*. Chicago: University of Chicago Press, 2019

9—Frazer, James George. *The Golden Bough* (1890). New York: Macmillan, Jan. 1, 1958

10—Strauss, William, and Howe, Neil. *The Fourth Turning: An American Prophecy*. New York: Crown, 1997

11—Start at https://lithub.com/looking-to-nurture-your-artistic-self-go-on-an-artist-date/

12—For a business example, see Harden, Jim, and Dude, Brad. *What Makes You Tick and What Ticks You Off*. Snow in Sarasota Publishing, 2009

13—Atchley R.A., Strayer, D.L., and Atchley, P. "Creativity in the Wild: Improving Creative Reasoning through Immersion in Natural Settings." *PLoS ONE* 7(12): e51474 (2012). https://doi.org/10.1371/journal.pone.0051474; Chowdhury, Madhuleena Roy. "The Positive Effects of Nature on Your Mental Well-Being." *PositivePsychology.com*, July 7, 2021. https://positivepsychology.com/positive-effects-of-nature; Huynh, Lam Thi Mai, et al. "Linking the Nonmaterial Dimensions of Human-Nature Relations and Human Well-Being Through Cultural Ecosystem Services." *Science Advance*s, 8:31 (August 2022). https://www.science.org/doi/10.1126/sciadv.abn8042

14—Hobson, Nicholas M., Schroeder, Juliana, et al. "The Psychology of Rituals: An Integrative Review and Process-Based Framework." *Personality and Social Psychology Review* 22:3 (2018), pp. 260-284;

Brooks, A.W., Schroeder, J.R., et al. "Don't Stop Believing: Rituals Improve Performance by Decreasing Anxiety." *Organizational Behavior and Human Decision Processes* 137, pp. 71-85; Tian, A.D., et al. "Enacting Rituals to Improve Self-Control." *Journal of Personality and Social Psychology* 114, pp. 851-876. https://doi.org/10.1037/pspa0000113; Berinato, Scott. "The Restorative Power of Ritual." *Harvard Business Review*, April 2, 2020. https://hbr.org/2020/04/the-restorative-power-of-ritual

15—Carson, Shelley. "The Unleashed Mind." *Scientific American Mind*, 22: 2 (2011), pp. 22–29. http://www.jstor.org/stable/24943311

16—Matthews, Gail, "The Impact of Commitment, Accountability, and Written Goals on Goal Achievement." *Dominican Scholar*, 2007 https://scholar.dominican.edu/psychology-faculty-conference-presentations/3; Schippers, M., Scheepers, A., and Peterson, J. "A Scalable Goal-Setting Intervention Closes Both the Gender and Ethnic Minority Achievement Gap." *Palgrave Commun* 1:15014 (2015). https://doi.org/10.1057/palcomms.2015.14

PART 2:

Putting the Seasons to Work

Spark New Creation in Spring

It's hard not to like spring. This season earns the title of "favorite" for many people—more than a third in some surveys. (Kids prefer summer for obvious reasons, and the results of other surveys favor fall instead—especially when people are asked in late summer.)[1] Longer days, a warming Earth, and new growth prompt cheer. The fickle sun has clearly returned to support us, so spring is associated with sunrise, the eastern horizon, and, by inference, inspiration—the dawning of new light and new ways of seeing. In addition, of course, sprouting plants, unfurling leaves, and baby animals made spring and sunrise our fundamental metaphors for new creation millennia before the invention of light bulbs lent us that electric symbol for new ideas.

Spring energies in brief: *Inspiration, generation, discovery, rebellious innovation, discernment, and tolerance for foolishness.*

Every season is a time of transition, but human beings have a bias for life and optimism. As a result, the transition from winter's apparent death to new life stands out from the other seasons in significance. Winter may still have a grip, but hoped-for change becomes evident in melting ice, warming breezes, swelling plant buds, and nesting birds. The Earth stands on the threshold between a dark period of rest and a brighter one of growth in one of the more obviously in-between times of the year.

Transitional times like these are called liminal. The Latin root word, *lī'mən*, means threshold. Just as the threshold of a doorway separates indoors from outdoors or one room from another, metaphorical thresholds separate past and future, known and unknown, who we have been and who we will become.

Humans have deep-seated psychological associations with liminal places and times. They often make us uneasy or restless (as in spring fever). This mild anxiety is based in part on our instinctive fear of change and the unknown ahead, as well as the desire—once we've decided to cross any threshold—to get on with it and leave the old place behind.

But liminal spaces and times, including spring, are also hotbeds of creativity, beauty, opportunity, and riches. Think tropical beaches, both lovely and possibly yielding buried treasure, or the wonders on the far side of a magic portal. Such associations underscore the hope, growth, and innovation we attribute to spring.

The changes evident everywhere during this time of year can energize us toward inspiration, innovation, and creative fertility. But while these key themes and associations of spring seem obvious, it may be less obvious how to harness their energy for your creative work. Try the activities that follow in this section to put each concept into practice.

> *Don't wait for inspiration to strike—court it.*

How to put spring energy to work

▶ **Seek inspiration:** You're not as helpless as a seed awaiting the right combination of moisture and temperature, so don't fall into the trap of assuming that ideas arrive randomly and all you can do is wait. Creativity research suggests that historical constructs for "courting the muse" were correct, and we can create conditions more likely to result in ideas. So don't wait for inspiration to strike—court it with the activities called Conspire with Clouds (p. 64), Connect with Your Artistic Spirit (p. 66), Capture Sounds on Sticky Notes (p. 68), Cross-Pollinate (p. 70), and Explore Voice with Birdsong (p. 78).

▶ **Break loose to discover something new:** After being cooped up all winter, restlessness is so common we call it spring fever. It may be creative rather than hormonal, but spring fever can afflict artists, too. Embrace it. Rebel against a self-imposed barrier or expectation, forging new paths to innovate. What artistic constraints or conventional wisdom do you need to smash? What new direction is your heart pulling you toward? What's stopping you? (Hint: Fear of ridicule is a big one. But remember that innovators from Galileo to modern-day Nobel Prize winners were ridiculed before their genius was recognized. Read the next paragraph and then take the risk.) Break out with help from the activity called Open the Door (p. 76).

▶ **Get a little foolish:** The unpredictability of rapidly changing weather and spring's in-between status aligns the season with other manifestations of the Trickster, including practical jokes, erratic or transgressive behavior (think young people on spring break), and sudden windfalls or luck (St. Patrick's Day leprechauns and pots of gold). In fact, the energy of spring fever is often called foolishness—and the history of April Fool's Day is murky, but it's no coincidence that it happens on a liminal date near the start of the season and what was, for centuries, the start of the year. Take advantage of this temporary tolerance (and encourage it in yourself) with the activities called Break a Rule (p. 75) and Think Divergently (p. 80).

▶ **Sort and decide:** Although autumn is when humans sort food grains from the chaff, spring is when nature performs most of this sorting, identifying which seeds will sprout and which will decay into nutrients for something else. Spring-cleaning rituals are a human form of discernment, too, chasing out old cobwebs and putting away unneeded sweaters and boots. Finally, discernment is required to distinguish spring foolishness from true innovation.

These influences make spring a great time to use Sweep Clean (p. 86) to revisit old ideas or half-completed projects and decide whether they warrant more work, should be shelved for a more appropriate time later, or need to be tossed on the compost pile of experience. The activity called Inhale and Exhale to Create (p. 83) can also sharpen your discernment.

Rebel against a self-imposed barrier or expectation.

▶ **Give ideas material form:** From the sparks of a new fire to a sprout bursting from a formerly inert seed, spring is all about birthing into existence something not there before—turning spirit or symbol into something tangible and converting ideas into a material work of art, even if it is immature. You can practice making the symbolic tangible with Find a Project Talisman (p. 59), or kick off a project or working session with the activity called Step over a Threshold (p. 61). The threshold activity is also a great way to commit to a full year of creative exploration with this book.

Finally, capitalize on spring energy by producing. Spring is a great time for intense bursts of work. Put this book down as needed to try "fast drafting," or complete a challenge to create every day for a month. Popular challenges of this type are National/Global Poetry Writing Month, aka Na/GloPoWriMo, and the idea-generation blast now called Storystorm.[2] If you miss their official timing—April and January, respectively—you can still use the concept. Just create your own progress reporting or support network informally in your creative community or on social media.

Spring is a great time for intense bursts of work.

Spring activities that follow:

Find a Project Talisman 59
Step over a Threshold 61
Conspire with Clouds 64
Connect with Your Artistic Spirit 66
Capture Sounds on Sticky Notes 68
Cross-Pollinate 70
Break a Rule 75
Open the Door 76
Explore Voice with Birdsong 78
Think Divergently 80
Inhale and Exhale to Create 83
Sweep Clean 86

Find a Project Talisman

How this can help you: Practice the symbolic thinking of art, tease out fears and hopes to help overcome challenges, and gain a tangible reminder for motivation.

Many people are familiar with the idea of talismans, which are artifacts imbued with magic to confer special powers or talents or provide supernatural guidance. They appear everywhere in human cultures, from religions and myths—the Golden Fleece, the Holy Grail—to popular fantasy tales and video games. Well-known examples range from the Seven-League Boots to the One Ring in J.R.R. Tolkien's *The Lord of the Rings*.

Talismans are usually created objects, but exceptions range from a certain goose's golden egg to four-leaf clovers. Talismans often have symbolic as well as magical powers. The One Ring, for example, is arguably a ring (and not, say, a pendant or brooch) because the circle of a ring represents unity, as in "to bind them" and ruling all. King Arthur's Sword in the Stone conferred leadership in a culture that assumed physical force, if not violence, was required. (There's a reason he didn't become king by successfully donning magical socks.)

Why this activity fits spring: *It aligns with spring's associations with discovery and symbolic thinking.*

It's through symbolism that we grant power to everyday talismans. But that power can be real. Just as Super Mario gains strength with a Super Mushroom, a natural talisman for your creative work can help you persevere through the challenges that all artists face.

Use the following activity to identify one.

Find a Project Talisman—Step by Step

You'll need: Your phone/camera or a sketchbook, a pen, and 20–30 minutes.

1. **Get outdoors** with your phone, camera, or sketchbook in your pocket and your current project in mind.
2. **Look for a meaningful natural talisman** for your project. Let your mind free-associate as you notice natural items around you, from tree bark to clouds, and consider meaningful symbolism you might grant them. Try to think beyond obvious candidates such as an acorn or other seed that represents the larger possibility your work will mature into.
3. **When you spot (or hear or smell) something that appeals, consider it closely.** Take a photo or sketch it from a couple of angles, or pick it up if that's safe and appropriate.

Wildly Inspired

4. **Answer the following questions** for yourself in a journal. Refer to the examples below as needed. If you're drawn to something you don't know much about—or even what it is—Google and the Google Images reverse search can usually help.

- What is the item (if you know)? *Example: A small stick of driftwood.*
- Which of this item's traits appeal to you? List several. *Example: Smooth, worn soft, surprisingly light weight, intriguing curves, mystery of where it came from and how.*
- What are the strengths of this item, from either a survival or an aesthetic perspective? *Example: Washed up safely after a turbulent journey; soft, comforting to touch; deceptively light and easy to carry; dried out enough to float again.*
- How long does it take for this item to be created or come into existence? What forces can change it, and how readily? *Example: A long time in multiple stages: growing as a tree, falling into water, tumbling in waves, probably also broken or burned.*
- How can one or more of those strengths or other traits apply to your work or project? *Example: Multiple steps in the journey, like drafts, resulted in smoothness; no idea how long the journey might take; doesn't have to be a "heavy" topic to be pleasing.*
- What are a few of this item's weaknesses? *Example: Dead, not growing. Not very useful, doesn't make good firewood, washed up randomly rather than according to any plan.*
- How might those weaknesses also apply to your work—and what strategies could you take to mitigate them? *Example: Make sure I keep it lively, not flat/dead/boring. Could be too meandering, so—clearly establish my purpose and stick to it and get early feedback to be sure direction is clear.*
- If you anthropomorphized this item, what might it say to you about its own journey or yours? *Example: "Hey, it's okay if the journey takes a long time and you feel like you're sometimes drowning. But you're not 'washed up!' You just haven't arrived yet. Eventually you'll rest, smooth and gleaming, on a sunny shore."*

5. **Bring the power of your talisman into your workspace.** If it's small, take it home (assuming it's not anything you can't ethically remove from its home). Better yet, leave it there but post a photo or sketch of it near where you work.

6. **Extra challenge: Repeat this activity with a different item that jumps out because it's scary or repulsive.** (We can often learn more from negative reactions to things that are, after all, part of life.)

For example, when I first tried this activity, mud struck me as the right artifact. At first I resisted. Soggy dirt? Ugh! Couldn't I do better than that? But at that time, my project felt murky and a bit overwhelming, and the mud made me admit it: I was struggling with structure and clarity. Yet the more I thought about mud, the more I felt the power of that symbolism—because mud is often quite fertile, teeming with hidden life, and mudflows, known as lahars, are both energetic and influential. Mud records the passage of animals and insects to reveal history and teach us about ourselves and our world. Finally, with stillness and time, the mud settles and puddles clear... and intuitively I knew patience and a certain quiet listening was what my project needed so I could see it more clearly and be surprised by the newts or pollywogs—creative growth in action—hidden but waiting to emerge.

Step over a Threshold

How this can help you: A threshold ritual signals your subconscious that you're making an important change, which in turn can help you prioritize your work.

When I was a teen firmly committed to independence, I had no interest in marriage—except for one old-fashioned wedding ritual. I wanted to be carried over a threshold.

Looking back, I understand that impulse better, and not only because I eventually married. My longing to be helped through a symbolic crossing was probably driven by the nature of adolescence itself.

Teens are caught between childhood and adulthood in an uncomfortable spot that's neither one nor the other. Getting over that liminal threshold to adult independence appeals. But without a clear sense of how to get there, my subconscious wished for decisive assistance. (And yes, my groom kindly obliged me, well after I'd qualified as a grown-up, and we laughed, but the gesture still felt meaningful. Which is partly why I explored thresholds and in-between spaces in a master's thesis many years later.)

Why this activity fits spring: *It draws on spring's associations with discovery, physical expression of ideas, and the possibilities of a liminal space.*

The idea of crossing a threshold to a new adventure, new discoveries, and a new role or identity is also central to both the hero's journey and the artist's journey. (See "The Seasonal Cycle of the Hero's Journey" in Part 1.) Thresholds and images of thresholds have power; consider the many great paintings that include a doorway or window because of their dynamism and symbolic value, from da Vinci's *The Last Supper* to Chagall's *Window*. This symbolism also gives meaning to theatre prosceniums and the frames of paintings, both of which represent a threshold the viewer is asked to mentally step through into the world of the painting or play. And for art that remains intentionally unframed, that lack of a distinct boundary may be part of the point.

We can use this innate psychology of thresholds to our advantage. First, as artists, we can intentionally create a threshold that represents a new project, phase, or creative exploration. Crossing that threshold with purpose and ritual can nudge our subconscious into recognizing the change and behaving accordingly, focusing more on the project by accepting it as part of our new identity. Second, we can use thresholds in our work to incorporate their symbolic and psychological implications.

Consider this activity when you're starting a new project or exploration or want to embark on a revision of an old one.

Step over a Threshold—Step by Step

You'll need: A journal, pen, and 30–45 minutes, though you may decide to also bring something else in Step 2. You may also want your phone camera.

1. **Identify the project or exploration you're embarking on** and go somewhere with relative privacy, preferably outside. Embarking on a new adventure is self-conscious enough without strangers' eyes on your back.
2. **Consider what tools or magic you're bringing with you.** The trappings of the hero's journey can be a helpful reference. You might carry a small, meaningful object; a slip of paper with a few words that represent the strength or support you'll rely on; or a new pen or art media, for instance.
3. **Hold your project in mind** as you move through space. Look for suggestions of thresholds, gates, curtains, or doorways—or ways to make them—and **identify a threshold with meaning for you**, your project, or a character in it. Consider drooping branches to duck under, soil or sand you could draw on with a stick, or natural features such as creeks, stepping stones, or logs you could step onto, hop, or jump down from. If you're tackling a whole new direction, perhaps a twist or a 90-degree turn should be involved.
4. **Once you've found your threshold, decide how you'll cross it.** Plan to make it a ritual, not a mundane movement. Ideas include taking a specific number of steps, repeating a mantra, briefly closing your eyes, raising your fists in a victory salute, circling three times before crossing, etc. If you have trouble, borrow from familiar rituals: wedding bouquets or music, blowing out candles, flipping graduation caps into the air.
5. **Briefly sanctify your threshold.** Spend a few moments removing distractions such as dead leaves, twigs, or litter. Make any improvements you'd like (such as drawing shapes on the ground or lining a path to the threshold with sticks, stones, or flower blossoms). And be sure to confirm that you will be safe on both sides (and not, for instance, tripped by loose debris).
6. **Decide if you'll want a memento.** If so, arrange it to be easy to grab. This might be a selfie as you pass through the gate or a pebble lifted from a stone cairn as you pass, for instance. You can keep it near your workspace as a reminder.
7. **Pause on the "before" side of your threshold.** Become aware of your breath and hold your project in mind.
8. **Using the ritual you planned, cross over.** Don't look back. Your only path is forward.
9. **Answer these questions** in your journal:
    - Did you quickly make do with a ready, easy threshold, such as stepping off your porch or through a garden gate? Or did you take time to find or construct a threshold? The answer might reflect your commitment level (or your impatience with this activity).

- What hidden significance can you see in the type of space or materials you chose? Were they organic, inorganic (such as stones), flexible or rigid, dark colors or light?
- Did you step over, under, through, or around something? What significance might you find in that motion?
    + For instance, *stepping over* suggests rising over a hurdle and emphasizes your agency as you move forward. Your goals probably feel realistic. Are they too low?
    + *Stepping beneath* something (such as an overhanging branch or a traditional wedding arch) implies you expect to be in a completely different space moving forward because it better mimics a doorway between two separate places or roles, such as indoors and out. You may be anticipating change in yourself or your life, not merely your work.
    + *Stepping through* something or arranging a complicated threshold can imply a subconscious "eye of the needle" attitude. The challenge looks big and you're not sure you can do it. In retrospect, that's how I felt when, enacting a threshold for writing this book, I climbed into the fork of a tree to slip between the two halves. But take heart—the effort you put into the threshold also indicates high commitment that will drive you forward.
    + *Stepping around* an object such as a tree—maybe more than once—suggests uncertainty about which direction to go or where the project will lead you. Perhaps the journey will even be circuitous, but remember the cycle of the hero's journey, and fear not!
- How did you feel, emotionally and in your body, about the ritual itself? *(For instance, did you have any sense of unease or embarrassment?)* How much of that was about the ritual itself and how much about committing to the project?
- How might you incorporate a threshold—literal or figurative—into your current project? Could you also incorporate any of the feelings or sensations above into your work?
- What small threshold ritual might be useful to incorporate into your regular creative process? *For instance, it could help you leave the day's cares behind and access a more creative frame of mind if you pause each time you approach your workspace to gaze out a window before mentally moving through the window frame into your creative work.*

10. **For storytellers:**
    - What threshold does your protagonist cross early in their journey? (Note that an inciting incident and the moment the character crosses the threshold are typically not the same. For instance, Gandalf's arrival is the inciting incident for Bilbo Baggins in *The Hobbit*, but he doesn't cross the threshold until he leaves his house to follow the dwarves.)
    - What threshold(s) has your protagonist crossed before your story starts, and what happened? How might that experience affect their attitudes at the threshold in your story?
    - How might you use any of your answers or insights in Step 9 in your work?
11. Over time, refer to any memento you took as a **reminder of your commitment** to yourself.

Conspire with Clouds

 *How this can help you:* Activate your brain's default network to stimulate creative ideas and your access to them.

One windy spring morning while walking my dog, I stopped and sat on a log to watch threatening clouds racing past, intrigued by their unusually ragged, dark aspect and how they churned nearer and nearer the ground. A few swept over me as wet currents of fog. The air was so full of water that, although rain didn't fall, visible streams of mist unfurled on the wind.

Why this activity fits spring: *In most climates, spring weather prompts interesting clouds, and mind-wandering promotes new growth and ideas.*

Suddenly the grey swirls coalesced into white dots. Curtains of snow began blowing around me, the flakes cascading one moment, spinning, floating upward, and plunging back down.

The wind-driven snow stung my cheeks and stuck in my lashes, and I was soon soaked and chilled. But it was too amazing to flee. I tipped my head further back and got lost in the sky, which had dropped to surround me. Not gentle, this snow, the flakes swelled to pour down, shrank to graupel, then grew fluffy again. A maelstrom of texture and motion.

I can't promise excitement like this, but a lazy session of watching clouds is almost certain to help calm your body and mind, both prerequisites for creative work. It engages your brain's default network, which links multiple areas of the brain during relaxation, when the mind is idling or directed internally—such as on memories—rather than focused on a specific external task or stimulation. The default network, which becomes active during mind-wandering, is associated with creativity. Creativity also seems to depend on connections between that default network and other areas more responsible for conscious, directed thought.[3] One way to strengthen those connections is to let your mind wander, but observe where it goes. You may not find a solution to a current creative problem, but time spent gazing at clouds will strengthen your ability to find one in the future. This activity is also a good prelude to the next one, Connect with Your Artistic Spirit.

One caution: Pick a different activity if you're feeling gloomy or sad. Although the research is not conclusive,[4] activating the default network when you're already feeling low could make your mood worse.

Conspire with Clouds—Step by Step

You'll need: 20–30 minutes, a phone or kitchen timer, a journal, and a pen.

1. **Pick a comfy location where you can see the sky.** You can do this though a window, if the weather's unpleasant. But if possible, sit or lie on the ground where you can relax.
2. **Set a timer for at least 12 minutes**. Twenty would be better. You need to take long enough to stop thinking about what you forgot earlier or what you need to do next. As long as your mind is churning, your default network's not active, so have your journal and a pen handy to jot down anything pressing that will otherwise prevent you from relaxing. The timer will ensure you won't fall asleep and can get to that to-do list soon enough.
3. **Let your breath deepen and slow**. **Watch the clouds** with your mind as loose as possible. Our pattern-matching brains can hardly resist finding shapes, but try to only observe. If you're feeling playful, imagine what a given cloud tastes, smells, or feels like.
4. **When the timer goes off, consider these questions**, using your journal to capture useful answers or insights.
    - How does letting your mind wander make you feel? If it seems like a waste of time, who or what in your past sent you that message, and why?
    - Notice the impermanence of the clouds. What in your creative life is enduring? What has changed shape or been more fleeting? (Both have value.)
    - Notice whether your clouds are all the same type, height, color, texture, or density, and whether they hold still, all move in unison, or drift in different directions or at varying speeds. Do you find yourself longing for more stability and uniformity or more variety in your projects and practice? How could you satisfy that longing?
    - Since Earth is essentially a closed system, some of the air and water molecules in those clouds have been inside you as your own moisture-laden breath. Others will be in the future. How do you feel about this relationship? Where else might those molecules have once been? (*A far-away land, inside a dinosaur?*) How might you reflect such connections in your work?
    - If you're a storyteller, would your main character take time to watch clouds? If they did, what would happen? Or is there something else in their life—a fish tank, wind in trees, a bubble machine—that might offer a similar experience? How might it influence their emotions, decisions, or actions?
5. **Take this sense of spacious calm into the rest of your day.** If you have a eureka moment, great. But don't expect one. This is brain yoga that will pay creative dividends over time.

Connect with Your Artistic Spirit

 *How this can help you:* Clarify how your work fits into a larger context to elevate its priority in your life and help buoy you through rejection, fatigue, or challenges.

Across cultures, breath is the vehicle not only for life but for ideas. The word inspiration itself comes from the Latin word *inspīrāre*, which means to breathe in or on. Respiration uses the same root word—*spīrāre*. Similarly, the Sanskrit word *prana* represents not only the breath but the life force itself and its manifestation as creative energy. Because air carries sound as well as life itself, it's no wonder that famous artists and authors such as Percy Bysshe Shelley described their work as blowing to them on divine or mystical winds.

Why this activity fits spring: *Spring is the season of rising spirits, new life and ideas, spirited breezes, and spirituality in general.*

Listening quietly to the breeze is still one of the best ways to court ideas and insight. Being still also raises awareness of our own spirituality, which transcends religion or beliefs as our connection to something larger than ourselves. You get to decide what that larger thing is; purpose, community, art, and values are popular choices that sit comfortably along any sense of the Divine.

Try this activity to gain insight into what stirs you to create and how your art nurtures your spirit. Focusing on how your art fits into your life and the experience of being human can buoy you through difficult times as well as provide the foundation for statements of artistic purpose and branding activities.

Connect with Your Artistic Spirit—Step by Step

You'll need: A comfortable spot with a breeze, a pen, and a journal, and about 30 minutes.

1. **Get comfortable somewhere with a natural breeze**—outdoors or near an open window. (The cloudwatching activity immediately before this one would be great preparation.)
2. Inhale deeply. **Allow your breathing to slow.**
3. **Watch how the air moves** around you, possibly fluttering grass, trees, or curtains.
4. Close your eyes. Listen and **notice the movement of air on your skin, at your nostrils, in your lungs**. If the air seems perfectly still, raise your awareness of the air pressure on your cheeks or passing into your nostrils, or the tiny breeze your own exhalation can create on your raised palm. Or can you hear distant wind you can't feel?

5. **Visualize the air molecules outside of you becoming part of you,** as well as how molecules from inside depart on your exhalations to interact with the world. As you listen, can you hear or feel your heartbeat? Other thoughts intruding?
6. Now, continuing to listen inside and outside, **answer these questions** in your journal:
    - We honor what we consider sacred. What aspects of your impulse to create, if any, do you feel are sacred? *(For instance, the drive to create or to bring joy or meaning to others.)*
    - What changes in your answer, if anything, if your work is not "commercial" or nobody else "likes" it? Why or why not?
    - How do you think of your work's role in your life? Read slowly through this alphabetical list and circle or note any that feel appropriate for you:

        Activity, aspiration, calling, career, challenge, charity, community, contribution, dharma, distraction, duty, entertainment, expression, fun, game, hobby, identity, inspiration, joy, obligation, obsession, pastime, path, play, practice, prayer, purpose, social connection, waste of time, worship, other: _____

    - Given the words you chose, how could changes in your attitude, work habits, or the work itself enable you to achieve more satisfaction?
    - What words from the list did you not circle but might want to explore more in the context of your work?
    - Name one activity or habit in your life that takes time from your work but does not meet the standards of the words you circled. (Social media and TV are likely responses.) How might you shift time or attention from that lower priority to your work?
    - Rituals can confer meaning and help create the right mindset. What rituals, if any, do you have around your work? *(For example, a mandatory beverage or activity before getting started, or what you do with work after it's completed or abandoned.)*
    - Rituals can also enable procrastination or prevent work because the ritual is impossible or conditions aren't "just right." How do your rituals help or hinder your work? What change might be useful in that regard?
    - This activity should make you want to go work. If it hasn't, why not? What could you do about that?
7. If you like, **write the most important words you circled above onto sticky notes** and post them in your work area. When you're struggling, they can remind you why you're a writer or artist.

Capture Sounds on Sticky Notes

 *How this can help you:* Increase sensory awareness, incorporate it into your work, and strengthen your ability to symbolize the intangible.

Chittering birds are not the only notes of spring's symphony. In some places, the percussive drip of melting ice may signal spring. In others, the roar of the first lawnmowers drowns out everything else. Whatever kind of soundscape surrounds you, paying more attention to it is a fun spring activity that can surprisingly sharpen all your senses. When we relax the tyranny of our sight, other senses can come to the fore.

Why this activity fits spring: *Like new life, it makes the intangible tangible and it draws inspiration from (airborne) sound.*

Some people find this activity challenging; others are surprised by emotions or memories that surface. In one example, a workshop participant took her sticky notes into a meadow and sat in her shorts on the grass. She caught sounds as intended but was struck harder by the tactile sensation of grass pressed into and marking the skin of her calves. Childhood memories and emotions rushed back to her. Knowing the value of such specific and authentic details, she immediately began capturing them in her journal to incorporate them into her current project.

This activity is most useful or revealing for those who aren't skilled at drawing. (If you are, challenge yourself not to rely on literal representations simply because you can.) It can also be fun to do with a group, comparing the various results for the same sounds.

Capture Sounds on Sticky Notes—Step by Step

You'll need: A block of sticky notes, your phone or a kitchen timer, a journal or sketchbook, 20–30 minutes, and one or more colored pens or pencils.

1. **Find somewhere outdoors where you can sit or stand comfortably for 15 minutes.** Try an unexplored corner of a park or a seldom-visited cranny of your yard, such as between the trash can and the fence. Or stick your head out a window where you don't usually linger, such as in a bathroom or garage.
2. **Set your phone timer to 7 minutes and stay still** the whole time, simply listening. If you're somewhere safe enough—no straying cars, thugs, or baseballs—closing your eyes can help you focus on sound.
3. On sticky notes, **jot down, by name or brief description, every sound you hear** during that time.

4. Set your phone timer to 7 minutes again and **visually capture at least three of your sounds, one sticky note each**. Use whatever marks, drawings, symbols, squiggles, colors, etc. you like, but avoid words. The idea is to make imaginative leaps from one sense (hearing) to another (visual) without the interface of language. Can you indicate volume, tone quality, intrusiveness, direction, motion, etc.? You'll have to work fairly quickly and instinctively, but if you have time, you can do one for every sound you heard.

5. Either in place or at home with your sticky notes, **answer these questions** in your journal:
    - Were there any sounds you didn't recognize or know the source of? How did those make you feel?
    - Why did you choose the sounds you decided to draw? If expedience or ease was a factor, how might that have bearing on your creative work?
    - Did you notice mostly pleasant or unpleasant sounds? Which did you draw?
    - How did your other senses (touch, scent) respond? What competed for your attention?
    - If you found this activity difficult, why? How might it reflect any habitual challenges or tendencies in your work? *(For instance, if you wanted to draw literally and were frustrated by your drawing skill level, do you need to practice less literal and more symbolic thinking in general?)*

6. Finally, **choose just one of your sound drawings** and consider these questions, journaling the answers if you like:
    - What memories or emotions do you associate with this sound?
    - What connection is there, if any, between those memories or emotions and how you captured the sound visually?
    - What made you choose the marks you put on your sticky note for that sound? Is the result a literal drawing of an object or scene, a known symbol, an invented symbol, more of a scribble, something else?
    - Is that choice reflected in any way in your creative tendencies overall?
    - If you used different colors for different sounds, what's the connection for you between this sound and your chosen color(s)?
    - How can you incorporate this specific sound, a memory associated with it, or more sound generally, into your work, whether literally, symbolically, or emotionally? There's probably a way (even if your audience isn't conscious of it). For instance, if you're a storyteller, is there a place for this sound and a related memory or emotional reaction from your main character? Try writing such a scene to see what you might learn about the character and their background. Or if you're a visual artist, is there anything in the style or energy of your sticky-note image that you might incorporate into a current project?

Cross-Pollinate

How this can help you: Combining what initially seem like unrelated topics increases your cognitive disinhibition, which opens your mind for new ideas and connections.

Creativity experts talk about the role of cognitive disinhibition in breakthrough ideas.[5] Essentially, our brains make time-saving shortcuts that tell us cottage cheese has nothing to do with your car floor mats, for instance. We're inhibited from thinking about them together as a solution to a problem, whether that's cleaning the mats or how to eat lunch. In many cases, those shortcuts are correct. (I'll let your imagination fill in various bad ideas combining cottage cheese and floor mats.)

Why this activity fits spring: *It draws on spring's associations with inspiration, innovation, and new creation.*

But originality is all about making new and unexpected connections. We wouldn't have Velcro® today if inventor George de Mestral hadn't considered the stickiness of burdock burrs along with how to keep shirts or pants fastened. Forcing yourself to consider such odd-couple matches helps silence the mental filter that normally declares one thing has nothing to do with another. That way, you can make new connections and unexpected ideas.

Try the activity below to prompt new ideas, either for new approaches to your various creative pursuits or to resolve weaknesses or challenges of a specific project. Some of the results may be silly, but think of it as creating sparks by striking one thing against another. The result might be a new creative fire.

Cross-Pollinate—Step by Step

You'll need: Only a pen, this book, and 30–45 minutes. Or replicate the Mash-Up Matrix grid on p. 72 using bigger paper for more room to write.

1. **Spend a few minutes in a location you can enjoy.** I'll always recommend somewhere in nature, but if you're a storyteller, you might also visit an indoor setting with relevance for a current project, such as somewhere your character would go. Travel in your imagination if necessary. Notice a half-dozen intriguing images or sensations from those surroundings.

2. In the top row of your Mash-Up Matrix, **note those key nature or setting elements or images.** Refer to the examples on the next page.

3. **If you're seeking fresh ideas for a particular project,** in the first column of the matrix list a few characters, conflicts, or themes you're interested in or struggling with. (See the first example on the next page.) **If you're interested in expanding your creativity more generally**, list your current creative interests or projects instead. (See the second example.)

You might even mix both on the same matrix by, for instance, including a concern about a character's motivations as well as your own interest in learning a new creative skill.

4. Turn off that brain filter! **Pick an item in the first column and follow its row to each intersection with the nature or setting elements** listed across the top. *In the examples, follow "Parents' relationship" to its intersection with "Underground," or "Felting projects" to its intersection with "Moss."*

5. **Brainstorm ways to connect or explore the topic combinations at each intersection.** These might be minor references or a source of major inspiration. Refer to the examples as needed and note ideas at the intersections.

6. **Don't stop at the first idea.** Make a list and elaborate in a journal if more space is needed. Once you've pierced the mental filter, ideas will start to flow, and research shows that more ideas generally result in more originality.[6] The more you challenge yourself, the more likely you'll ignite a fresh idea worth exploring.

	Setting elements and images		
Characters, conflicts, theme	Underground	Restaurant	River
Parents' relationship	Argument at mouth of tunnel about secrets; flashback	Money concerns; public embarrassment; contrast food orders or ways of eating	Attitudes toward risks; bubbly vs. deep personalities; going with the flow or stuck in eddy

	Nature elements or images		
Creative pursuits	Moss	Cottonwood scent	My zebra cactus
Felting projects	Try adding moss strands; use as stuffing for 3D felting; felt a moss-colored bath mat; felt pouch-shaped birdhouse lined with moss; write story of elf who felts with moss	Add essential oils; make felted sachets for drawers; felt scented cottonwood leaves for Xmas ornaments (or other shapes!)	Felt mini plant pots; research wool as soil amendment; replicate zebra stripes in felt

	Nature or setting elements or images							
	Creative pursuits or characters, conflicts, theme							

7. After you run out of ideas for one combination, **make another pairing and brainstorm again**. Ideas for the first match-up may continue to surface; note them.
8. **Follow up on any sparks** by trying to work them into a current or new project. Often it's not the quality of the original idea but how much we're willing to work with and develop it that determines its ultimate success.
9. **Set the matrix aside and plan to return to it later.** It's easy to get bogged down in the many potential combinations, but you can work with the matrix only until you're moved to go try an idea. Come back to brainstorm more cross-pollinations another day, or even use the matrix as a kick-starter for each of your creative work sessions.
10. **Once you've got the idea, break loose** from columns and rows, too. You might consider the conjunction of two setting elements or two separate listings from your first column.

Wildly Inspired

2. Immediately **answer these questions** in a journal:
   - How did that rule-breaking make you feel emotionally? Physically?
   - What accepted rules in your creative life do you follow without question?
   - What rule in your creative life now chafes you the most? What purpose(s) does that rule serve? (For example, clarity, audience enjoyment, technical feasibility, avoid overused tropes.)
   - When or how could breaking this rule result in compelling work?
   - In what ways, if any, have you already tried to circumvent it? What happened?
   - What are you afraid will happen if you break it? How could you prevent or mitigate a negative result?

3. **Try breaking that rule** in a current project (or a copy of it, so you can protect the original as needed). How do you feel about the results? What have you learned?

4. **For storytellers:**
   - What rule does your character want (or need) to break, and why?
   - Whose rule is it, and what does the character think will happen if they do break it?
   - What's one *unexpected* thing that might happen in addition or instead?
   - What rule do *you* need to break with this project? Try it.

Break a Rule

How this can help you: Practice loosening self-imposed constraints to find inventive solutions and new approaches that can help make your work unique.

How uncomfortable—or delighted—did this upside-down spread make you feel? Were you compelled to flip the book over or turn another page to see if the pages continued to break the usual rules for orientation?

Rule-breaking is a well-recognized aspect of liminal times and spaces. Examples include Halloween's trick-or-treat shakedowns, anything-goes bachelor parties, tolerance of senior pranks, and acceptable dishonesty on April Fool's Day. Such disruptions of the established order go hand-in-hand with in-between times and the creativity and opportunity they represent.

Why this activity fits spring: Spring is the most liminal season, and rule-breaking is a key characteristic of liminal times (and often great art).

At the same time, most art pursuits are weighted with written and unwritten rules of the craft. You can probably list at least a dozen that apply to your creative field. Most of them exist for a reason, though that reason is not always obvious. Meanwhile, well-known quotations about learning those rules so you can break them are routinely—and falsely—attributed to eminences ranging from Pablo Picasso to the fourteenth Dalai Lama. There's good evidence[7] that neither of their so-called famous quotes on the subject came from them, but the misquotes propagate because we want to believe them. In fact, some research indicates that while constraints can encourage creativity, being willing to break rules is associated with higher creativity, too.[8] You can't come up with new ideas if you're forever conforming to old ones.

But we're conditioned from birth to follow most rules, and since the social price of breaking too many is high, most of us need practice in breaking a few. This activity will give you that practice while helping you become more conscious of your own tendencies to follow rules or break them.

Break a Rule—Step by Step

You'll need: This book, a journal and pen, and about 15 minutes.

1. In your local environment, **break a minor rule** while paying close attention to your thoughts, feelings, and bodily reactions. (Break a social norm, not a rule designed to keep you safe.) For instance, rip a leaf off a houseplant, lick your dog or cat, or smear dirt or food all over your face.

Spark New Creation in Spring

Open the Door

 *How this can help you:* Strengthen your imagination with visualization practice and create a virtual refuge you can return to for answers to challenges with your work.

If you read the Spring introduction, you know that liminal spaces are between one place or time and another. The uneasiness we may feel in such places comes in part because they're associated not only with creativity and opportunity but also with unknown threats, even monsters. (That's why ghosts materialize on stairways, gargoyles leer from cornices, and vampires appear at windowsills, for instance. Such locations are all in-between.)

Why this activity fits spring: *In addition to the season's association with discovery, spring is the most liminal (threshold) time of the year.*

My favorite liminal place from my childhood, which contained both monsters and treasures, was the creek that emerged from a giant culvert behind our apartment building and flowed into the woods. While any shore is a liminal space between water and land, this creek was better, though you'll shudder when I explain why: It was part of a storm sewer system apparently connected to our building's septic system—or at least that's what my friends and I believed. (Looking back, this seems unlikely, but it was the 1960s, before the environmental movement, and the horror on my mother's face when she found out where we played seemed to confirm our conviction.) The culvert gaped wide enough for us to walk into its mouth.

Playing at the entrance to this subterranean world, we dared each other farther into the dark, listened for the sound of flushing toilets, and ran screaming from the wet surges we imagined would follow. Regardless of the water's true source, all sorts of trash clogged the creek near the culvert, and the beer cans, soggy shorts, and occasional stolen bike were full of playtime potential. We searched among the litter for gold jewelry that could have been lost down a drain, and the polliwogs we found suggested the water wasn't as toxic as it sounds. Most importantly, we engaged our imaginations for hours, and I don't think it's coincidental that I wrote my first story that year. Creativity takes practice, and there's nowhere better to do it than in a liminal space.

Which is why I recommend the following activity. I promise it involves no sewers or trash but relies instead on the power of a different in-between place. Those willing to brave the doorway into another world can invite the liminal creativity of spring into conscious awareness from the sanitary safety of a chair or recliner.

Open the Door—Step by Step

You'll need: About 30 minutes, a journal or sketchpad, and the 22-minute meditation guidance I've recorded for you online at https://youtu.be/itVmO2xTDOs.

1. **Turn on the "do not disturb" feature of your phone** and eliminate any other distractions that are likely to interrupt.
2. **Sit or lie down and get as comfy as you can, with a pen in your hand and a journal or sketchbook** in your lap or close within reach. If possible, do this meditation outdoors, where the sounds and smells of the season can help. (But avoid somewhere with intrusive traffic or other mechanical noise; if that's an issue, visit nature in your imagination only.)
3. **Listen to the recorded meditation guidance** (online at the link above) and follow the instructions in the audio.
4. Once you've finished the meditation, **look back over everything you just put on paper**. It might be a mess, and that's okay. Add or elaborate on anything that arose in your visualization but that you didn't have time for during the recording.
5. Now, with the more analytical part of your mind, **answer the following questions** in your journal or on another page of your sketchpad:
   - What parts of your visualization surprised you?
   - Do any echo or connect with images, characters, or other elements of a current project? Or with each other?
   - What images, sensations, or feelings jumped out at you, confused or concerned you, or otherwise might be worth exploring more deeply?
   - What personal memories, emotions, or experiences rise when you consider each? Why?
   - How do you feel about possibly returning to that same creativity clearing? What would you hope or fear might be there next time?
   - How can you incorporate anything from this visualization—a symbol, an emotion, a plot twist—into your work?
6. Since guided meditations are a form of mild self-hypnosis, be sure to **do something active or analytical** between listening to the meditation and, for instance, driving.
7. **Repeat this activity if you like.** Visualization becomes easier with practice. Repetition also sends a signal to your subconscious that you're willing to hear from and work with it using this method. This can be a good way to find solutions to creative problems—awake or asleep! Try priming your dreams by revisiting and opening that door as you fall asleep. You may feel you've found an answer when you awake the next morning.

Explore Voice with Birdsong

 *How this can help you:* Foster a creative mental state, heighten awareness of artistic voice or style, and increase sensitivity to the use of sound in your work.

Birds use a variety of tweets, chirps, calls, and shrieks to talk to each other. Probably they're mostly saying, "Watch out for that hawk!" or "Hellooo, I'm looking for a girlfriend," and "Hey, the human finally filled the seed dish again." Remarkably, research shows that different species can often understand one other, despite the variations in their languages or voices. The acerbic, sometimes sarcastic crow and the pip-pipping hummingbird will say similar things in quite different ways.

Why this activity fits spring: *Breezes and the sounds that travel on them are emblematic of spring, and birds typically sing most actively on spring mornings.*

That makes bird calls a surprisingly helpful tool for developing an artistic voice or style—either your own or, if you're a storyteller, that of a character. After all, style amounts to a personalized manner of communicating that would mean the same but sound or look different if it came from someone else. This activity asks you to focus on birdsong to make the elusive aspects of voice more tangible and practice playing with them. It also heightens your sensitivity to sound in your creative work, even if there's nothing aural about it. (For instance, look up chromesthesia to see how some visual artists create musical paintings.[9])

Finally, simply listening to sounds of nature has repeatedly shown to improve mood, ease stress, and enhance brain function.[10] Regardless of your interest in style, you can use this activity to help yourself settle into a calm, creative frame of mind.

Explore Voice with Birdsong—Step by Step

You'll need: About 40 minutes, your ears, a pen, your phone or kitchen timer, and a journal. Optional: An Internet connection to about 2 minutes' worth of prerecorded birdsong at https://youtu.be/9r5a1yHqAmg.

1. **Find somewhere you can hear birdsong** without other distractions. Three choices:
   - ☐ Sit outside or near an open window or porch where you can tune out competing sounds.
   - ☐ Access the compilation I've recorded for you at https://youtu.be/9r5a1yHqAmg.
   - ☐ Use a nature-sounds app such as *MyNoises* or birdsong offerings on YouTube.
2. **Set a timer for 15 minutes.**

3. **Listen carefully** to a variety of birdsongs and calls. You needn't be able to name the birds. Just think of them as Voice A, B, C, etc. Draw your attention back each time it wanders.
4. For each, **jot a few notes about the bird's voice.** See the examples below. Include both objective descriptors and emotional tenor or personality implications, using your imagination as much as you like.

Voice # or bird name	Description of sound	Emotional tenor, other impressions
Jay	Harsh but cheerful squawk	Bold, brassy, screechy mother-in-law who loves to complain
Peeper #2	High, sweet ni-ni-ni-ni	Optimist, maybe naïve or even annoying, like a beloved but pesty little sister

5. As you listen, **consider the following questions** and note the answers in a journal if you like:
    - Over time, do you notice patterns, lulls, or shifts?
    - What other sounds, such as wind or traffic, accompany the birdsong?
    - If you're outside, what happens if you respond with a mimicked or different sound?
6. When your timer goes off, **internalize what you've heard** with one or more of the suggestions below:

    ☐ Pretend you're a new bird species and **come up with a chirp, click, whistle, or other sound sequence of your own** to express each of three different emotions, such as pride, loneliness, and alarm. Share these sounds with a family member or friend who won't laugh too hard and see if they can guess which sound goes with which emotion.

    ☐ **Write a poem that uses at least two of the sounds** you heard to evoke emotions or images.

    ☐ **Pick a distinct call and create something in that style.** Consider mood, rhythm, shape, patterns, word or color choices, line weight or intensity, level of detail, etc. For instance, draft a paragraph that might fit into a current writing project or sketch something in the style of the voice. If you have trouble, first try to move your body in a way that evokes that bird's sound and mood.

    ☐ If you're a storyteller, **identify a specific bird's voice for a key character**. If you know the bird, you might assign a few of its behaviors or mannerisms too, but the association need not be so overt. Simply keeping it in the back of your mind can help support you in giving them a characteristic voice.

7. **Consider how to include more sounds in your work**, literally or through their emotional qualities and movement.

Wildly Inspired

Think Divergently

 *How this can help you:* Have fun while strengthening an important component of creativity to increase the likelihood of creating original work.

In this era of predictive text, it's easy to enter a word or phrase in a search bar or text message to discover what people most frequently type next, whether it's what you intended or not. Predictive text relies on probabilities based on what people have actually typed in the past. If you type "art," for instance, the odds are good that the next word you plan to type might be deco, online, or supplies.

Why this activity fits spring: *The season celebrates innovation, deviation from norms, and new explorations.*

But what if you meant to type "sandwich" or "headache" next? That's divergent thinking—mental associations that depart, perhaps drastically, from the usual. By breaking assumptions, norms, and boundaries, divergent thinking is nearly the opposite of predictive text, which relies on the associations most commonly made by everyone else.

Psychologists consider divergent thinking a strong predictor of creativity.[11] Fortunately, it's a mental muscle you can strengthen. Meditation is one way. Another is by practicing with activities like this one, which is based on the tests psychologists use to measure divergent thinking. Try it with friends so you can be inspired by others' most surprising results.

Think Divergently—Step by Step

You'll need: 15 minutes, your phone or kitchen timer, a pen, and blank paper or a journal. Use colored pens or pencils if you like.

1. **Take a look at the basic shapes below and on the next page.** (Or collect your own shapes from nature and draw or trace them on blank paper.) Photocopy p. 81 or your shape page first if you'd like to repeat this activity, which is highly encouraged.

2. **Set a timer for 6–8 minutes.**

Spark New Creation in Spring

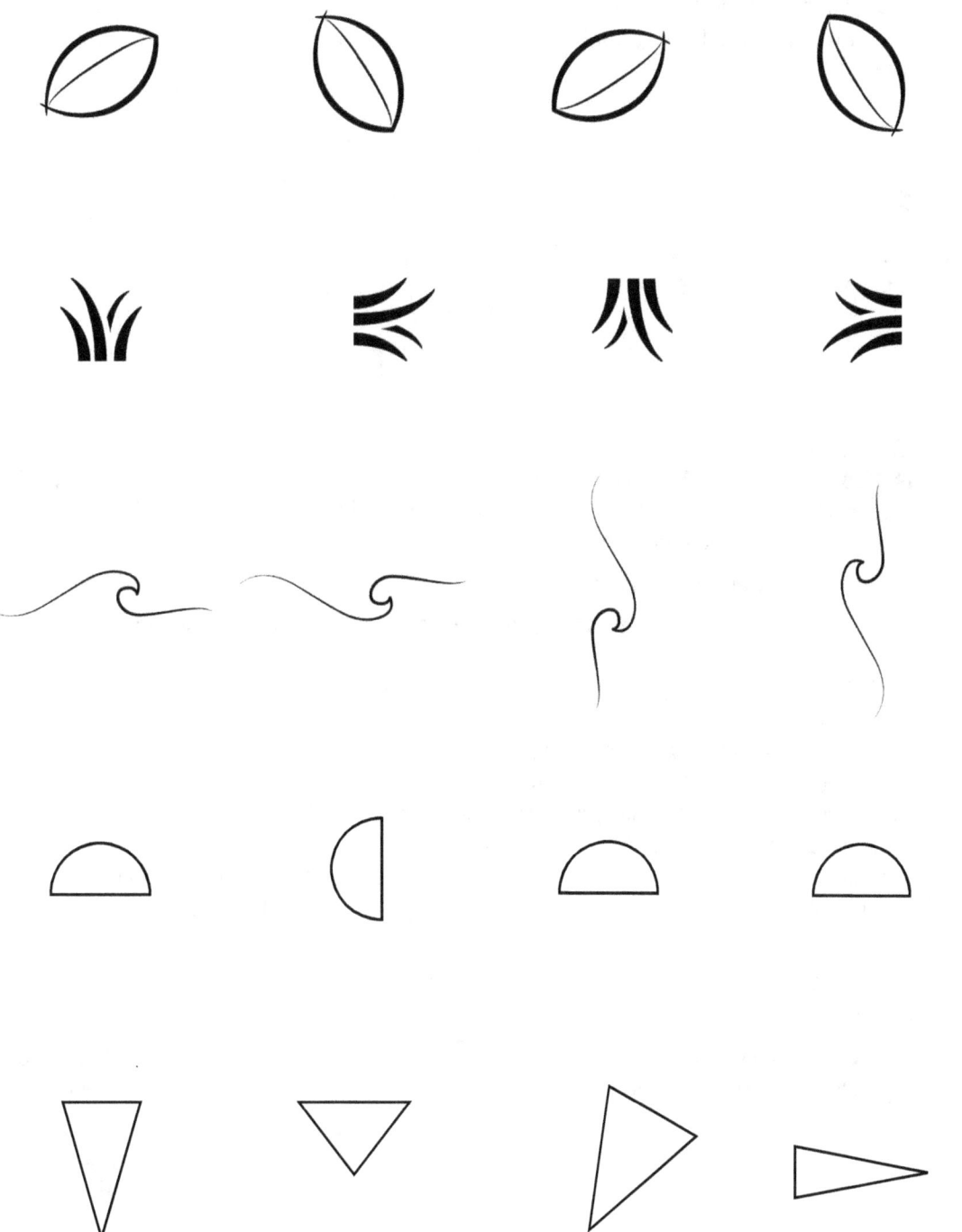

3. For each basic shape, **add to it to create something different**. (Refer to the examples below, which use the single row of shapes on p. 80.) As with brainstorming, don't think too hard or worry about drawing quality or accuracy. Work quickly; you have only seconds per drawing.

4. When the timer goes off, look back and **choose a few of your results that strike you as most surprising**. Mark them with stars or by circling them. If necessary, note in words what each is meant to be. If you like, take a minute to elaborate on or finish those drawings, or add color, titles, or funny captions.

5. **Answer these questions** in a journal.
   - What about your favorites stands out to you? What does the answer suggest about how your imagination works (or what you value)?
   - What themes or consistencies do you see? (*For example, you drew many faces or animals.*)
   - How varied are the scales or perspectives?
   - How much emotional content or humor is apparent?
   - How much movement or story links multiple images? Or did you incorporate more than one shape into the same drawing or scene?
   - Which images seem most unexpected? Were those near the start of the activity, in the middle, or toward the end? What does that suggest in terms of how long your creativity may take to warm up or wear down?

6. If you did this activity with others, **share your work**. What do you notice about your work, in terms of the journaling questions, compared with that of others?

7. Extra credit: In a journal, **create nine more drawings** that all use a single, identical image (which you'll need to draw first.) How many different things can you turn a single shape into?

Inhale and Exhale to Create

How this can help you: Heighten sensory awareness to bring specificity to your work and increase sensitivity to an innate rhythm that can help your audience connect.

As noted in the activity called Conspire with Clouds, air and breath are strongly associated with spring and inspiration. But the fundamental rhythm of breathing itself—the motion of air from outside our bodies to inside them and back—also appears in creative endeavors more often than many of us realize. It can be obvious in clearly rhythmic arts such as music or the contractive and expansive movements of dance. But even the strokes and lines of a visual art like painting have a rhythm, and rhythms also appears in less obvious art forms.

Why this activity fits spring: *Air, including breath and winds, is a key element of the season.*

For instance, successful writers sometimes consciously (and often unconsciously) rely on the rhythm of breathing in multiple ways. First, whether we're aware of it or not, syntax that follows the pacing of breath—or doesn't—is rooted in the fact that it's generally easier to read (even silently) when sentences match the length of a natural breath. Departures from that rhythm affect us. For instance:

- This run-on sentence you're reading now with fairly short words but not many pauses and nary a single comma can evoke a sense of breathlessness precisely because if you were reading it aloud you'd run out of breath before getting a chance to inhale.
- On the other hand, a meandering, extended sentence more like this one, conveniently peppered with clauses and commas, most of which allow you to pause, can feel leisurely to slow down the pace.
- Short fragments imply urgency. They convey "shortness of breath." The kind you have when you panic. Or get mad. Or excited. That builds tension. In scenes—and in readers.

This is one reason why writers are frequently advised to read drafts aloud. The ease and pace of our breathing while doing so are a good indicator not only of how challenging readers might find the syntax but also of whether the staccato or lilting pace and mood of the writing matches the scene's emotions.

Syntax is only one example of how creative work may imitate the rhythms of breathing. Try this activity to become more aware of ways your work can breathe. If you enjoy it, you might like to learn more about *pranayama* (breathing practices) and its impact on your parasympathetic nervous system, because activating that system can foster a mental state more conducive to creativity.

Inhale and Exhale to Create—Step by Step

You'll need: This activity is best done with a partner. You'll need 30–40 minutes, a timer, a pen, two blank pieces of paper, and a journal apiece.

1. **Sit comfortably, preferably somewhere less familiar than your home.** Get outside if you can. Give a blank paper to each partner. On it, create two columns; label one "inner" and one "outer." See the example below.
2. **Take five deep breaths,** exhaling for longer than you inhale. (For instance, inhale to a count of four and exhale to five.) Notice related sensations in your chest, belly, or nose.
3. **Start a 2-minute timer.** If you're alone, try 3 minutes instead.
4. Keep your eyes gently open but not looking around actively or at your partner. **Using all your senses, expand your awareness to your surroundings**—sounds, sights, sensations, smells, anything your closed mouth tastes like—and any emotions or internal sensations that arise.
5. If you have a partner, **call out everything you're aware of**, using just a few words for each. See the examples below. While listening only (no nodding or comments), your partner should **jot down each sensation** in the format below, deciding whether it's inner awareness (emotions, discomfort) or outer (sounds, sights). If you're alone, quickly note your own sensations and then direct your attention away from the pen and page.

Inner	Outer
Chest rising Self-conscious Hard chair Hungry	Sunlight from right Lawnmower nearby Scent of tea

6. **When time's up, switch who's aware and who's writing.** If alone, go to the next step.
7. **Swap pages, review your own sensations, and make corrections** in what's inner or outer if you like.
8. **Answer the following questions** in a journal and discuss with your partner, if you have one.
   - Do you have more internal or external impressions? What might this suggest about how you encounter the world?
   - What do you consider the "boundary" between inner and outer? Are skin sensations inside or outside? How about impressions colored by emotion, such as "annoying buzz"?

- Is the dominant theme, subject, or mood of your current project more internal or external? In other words, is your project heavy on action and movement, "quieter" and more focused on emotion, or—like breath—does it cycle between the two? How can you incorporate both in your work?
- In what other ways does the rhythm of breathing appear in your creative life? For instance, this might include periods of intense work followed by fallow times to "refill the well." Give yourself permission to embrace this natural rhythm.

9. Breathing pace significantly affects your nervous system. Slow breathing is likely to relax you and encourage internal sensations, while rapid breathing increases external focus. **Try repeating the activity starting with eight or 10 fast, short breaths** instead of five deep ones. (Take care not to hyperventilate.) Do you notice more external impressions, or does anything else feel different?

Extra credit for storytellers:

10. **If you did this exercise for a character, which column would dominate?** (If you don't know, try it—put them alone in a setting, imagine what they'd notice, and create a list for them.)
    - Where is the character's boundary, and how is it affected by gender, age, culture, or other factors?
    - How might you incorporate different tendencies or boundaries into the story, a conflict, or a character arc?

11. **Look at a representative scene** from one of your favorite books or your own writing. Notice which lines are more inwardly focused. (The balance will depend on the genre, target readership, and point of view, among other things. First-person narratives tend to have more interiority, for instance.) You might use two colors of highlighters to make the differences easy to spot.
    - Is there a lot more of one than the other? (Too much exteriority can make a scene feel emotionally distant. Interiority can generate tension, but when overdone may feel ungrounded, claustrophobic, or as though the tension never pays off.)
    - Is there a discernable rhythm of movement from inner to outer and back? How does it change toward the scene's climax?
    - Are there places where external references are used to express internal feelings? (What's known as the objective correlative[12] is only one of the ways to do this.) How might you use this idea to indicate that a character is intentionally or unintentionally avoiding their own internal awareness or feelings?

12. **Write (or rewrite) a scene** in your own work with attention to an inner/outer rhythm that encourages the effects you're after.

13. The larger rhythm of "scene and sequel" is another example of a breath-like movement from external (scene) to internal narrative or summary (sequel) and back. (If you're unfamiliar with the concept of scene and sequel, Google is your friend.) **How can you use this aspect of craft** to add more rhythm to your work?

Sweep Clean

 *How this can help you:* Reignite passion for a languishing project—or gain the confidence to say goodbye to a floundering one to free energy for more promising work.

Everyone thinks of new life in spring. We're less eager to examine the flip side of the coin, which is that renewal requires other possibilities to be discarded. Some seeds don't sprout or get crowded out. Some baby animals feed predators. We sweep out dead spiders during spring cleaning to clear corners for new ones (apparently). All of these losses make room for new growth.

Why this activity fits spring: *Discernment and sorting the strong from the weak is a seasonal strategy that makes room for new life.*

Creative projects need spring cleaning, too—especially the unfinished ones. When I was a kid, one of the phrases I memorized as part of the Blue Bird Wish was "Remember to finish what I begin." I've followed it almost to a fault. Similarly, many creatives feel a nagging sense that we "should" try to finish efforts we once loved that have stalled.

But sometimes letting go of an overworked project—acknowledging what it gave us in skills or experience and then moving it off the back burner and onto a shelf—serves our creative energies best. I now see the value of abandoning work. As spring reminds us, not everything needs to reach maturity. Back-burner pots that slowly boil dry can cause damage.

It's not only a matter of limited time. Incomplete projects drain psychic energy, and "should" is a constant reminder of avoidance and, on some level, failure. It erodes our confidence, thus the popular advice, "Don't should on yourself."

By contrast, choosing what *not* to work on frees energy. Spring, the time when latency's over, is ideal for this discernment and creative housecleaning. The biggest value of a creative project may come in honing skills that can be deployed more effectively elsewhere. Saying a final goodbye to a fatally flawed effort allows us to turn to something new and sparkling.

The trick, of course, is not to jettison a project that simply needs more incubation time, sharper skills, or a rekindling of your original passion for it. Try the activity below to make decisions—then act as you move into summer. It's inspired by a corporate problem-solving approach also used in the Autumn activity called Go Deeper with Five Whys. I used this process for years before discovering another writer who'd recognized its value. Author Naomi Kinsman has created a web app you can use, as of this writing, at https://www.naomikinsman.com/excavate-your-purpose-with-the-five-whys-game. Hers takes some twists from what you'll find below; try them both. They're helpful repeatedly over time, even for the same project in different stages of work.

Sweep Clean—Step by Step

You'll need: About 15 minutes, a journal, and a pen.

1. **Sit somewhere quiet where you won't be disturbed.**
2. **Identify a specific project** that needs examination. It may be one you're struggling with now or an old one that keeps calling to you.
3. **Answer all of the questions below as quickly as you can** to get at your instinctive reactions. The continued probing usually helps unearth more underlying or half-conscious issues. If you have trouble, the secondary questions may help guide you to answers.
   - Why did you first start this project? What sparked it or attracted you?
   - Why did it resonate or matter for you *personally and emotionally*? (That is, what in your life, background, or situation made the appeal especially significant for you?)
   - Why does it carry that emotional charge? (Why did it make you feel that way, and what is your history with the emotion or elements of the work?)
   - Why did you set this project aside or are tempted to do so now? (Why or how did you first begin having doubts or trouble? Why did that happen?)
   - Why was that reason sufficient? Why are the doubts or challenges stronger right now than the motivation?
   - Why haven't you already abandoned it for good? (What inside you is pushing you to keep going? Objectively, is that a good reason?)
   - How has this project already been valuable to you, directly or indirectly? What have you learned from it? (For example, it may have helped you develop skills or confidence, led to emotional insights, or entertained you.)
   - Why isn't that value enough to justify this project and allow you to move on permanently? (Or is it?)
   - How might you redirect the energy of your original inspiration into another project?
   - What have you realized as a result of this inquiry? How might that insight help guide you forward?
4. **Decide right now what will you do about this project moving forward.** The only real options include:
   - ☐ Do nothing and allow it to continue making you feel (consciously or unconsciously) unsuccessful. Not recommended.
   - ☐ Identify and take some concrete step to reactivate it by solving the source of the doubt or challenge. Good steps might include pulling it out to work on it, signing up for a class that would sharpen a skill you now see you need, or asking someone you trust to look at it and brainstorm with you about how to navigate around whatever's blocked. Note the step(s) you'll take in your journal.

- ☐ Draw on the original motivation to make an entirely fresh start on the project, with confidence that you've increased your skills since you started and therefore are in a better position to overcome the challenges you'll face in a new version.
- ☐ Thank it for what it taught you and let it go. Take a moment to say goodbye and mourn. Create a small ritual that will compost it back into future work. (If you must, you can simply put it away in a box or the garage in hope of a future resurrection, but squash any last "shoulds" associated with it.)

   A few examples:
   + *Find a natural object—a smooth stone, a leaf, a flower—that represents the project for you. Release it to a body of water.*
   + *Blow it along with soap bubbles or dandelion seeds into the breeze with a farewell or a wish for it to be taken up by someone better able to realize it.*
   + *Write the name or gist of your project on a leaf and bury it under a favorite plant, which can absorb and express the energy you've invested in it.*
   + *If you have somewhere safe to do so, write its name or gist on a piece of paper or wood and burn it, enjoying its transformation into pure energy that can reenter you and return in some other form.*

5. **If all your answers leave you unable to make that decision,** you probably haven't gotten to the heart of the issue. In that case, muse the questions and your answers (so far) on a walk, in the shower, or during a relatively mindless chore such as gardening or washing dishes. When your body is busy with activities like these, insights more readily bubble up.

Spring Endnotes

1—Survey results vary significantly depending on geographical region, climate, and even the respondents' race. Tastes also shift significantly as we age, and the oldest people favor spring most. In addition, results vary a lot depending on what time of year the survey takes place, with the upcoming season apparently having an edge. That is, fall is named the favorite at the end of summer, spring in January, and a single survey crowning winter took place near the end of autumn. YouGov.com survey, Jan. 23, 2024. https://today.yougov.com/topics/society/survey-results/daily/2024/01/23/56e6d/1; Jones, Jeffrey M. "Most Popular Season Coming to an End." Gallup News Service, *Gallup.com*, June 20, 2005. https://news.gallup.com/poll/16939/most-popular-season-coming-end.aspx; "Ipsos Poll: Favorite Seasons," *Ipsos*, Oct. 6, 2015. https://www.ipsos.com/sites/default/files/news_and_polls/2015-10/7014rev-topline.pdf; Davis, Maggie. "As Halloween Approaches, Americans Fall for Fall." ValuePenguin. Oct. 17, 2022. https://www.valuepenguin.com/travel/halloween-travel-survey; Briggs, Ellyn. "It's Official: Fall Is America's Favorite Season," *Morning Consult Survey*, Oct. 20, 2022. https://pro.morningconsult.com/instant-intel/fall-seasons-ranking

2—Check out opportunities at https://taralazar.com/storystorm/ or https://www.napowrimo.net. Although the original NaNoWriMo for novelists has died, find a good list of do-it-yourself tools at https://www.wisestamp.com/blog/best-tools-for-nanowrimo

3—Beaty, Roger E., et al. "Creativity and the Default Network: A Functional Connectivity Analysis of the Creative Brain at Rest." *Neuropsychologia* vol. 64 (2014): pp. 92-98. https://doi.org/10.1016/j.neuropsychologia.2014.09.019; Shofty, B., et al. "The Default Network Is Causally Linked to Creative Thinking." *Molecular Psychiatry* 27 (2022), pp. 1848–1854. https://doi.org/10.1038/s41380-021-01403-8

4—Konjedi, S., Maleeh, R. "A Closer Look at the Relationship Between the Default Network, Mind Wandering, Negative Mood, and Depression." *Cognitive, Affective, and Behavioral Neuroscience* 17 (2017), pp. 697–711. https://doi.org/10.3758/s13415-017-0506-z

5—Benedek, Mathias, et al. "Differential Effects of Cognitive Inhibition and Intelligence on Creativity." *Personality and Individual Differences*, 53:4 (2012), pp. 480-485. https:/doi.org/10.1016/j.paid.2012.04.014; Martindale, Colin, and Dailey, Audrey. "Creativity, Primary Process Cognition and Personality." *Personality and Individual Differences*, 20:4 (1996), pp. 409-414, https://doi.org/10.1016/0191-8869(95)00202-2.

6— Reiter-Palmon, R., and Arreola, N. J. "Does Generating Multiple Ideas Lead to Increased Creativity? A Comparison of Generating One Idea vs. Many." *Creativity Research Journal*, 27:4 (2015), pp. 369–374. https://doi.org/10.1080/10400419.2015.1087274; Johnson, B. R., and D'Lauro, C. J. "After Brainstorming, Groups Select an Early Generated Idea as Their Best Idea." *Small Group Research*, 49:2 (2017), pp. 177-194. https://doi.org/10.1177/1046496417720285

7—Specifically, https://www.snopes.com/fact-check/hello-dalai/

8—Petrou, Paraskevas, et al. "When Breaking the Rules Relates to Creativity: The Role of Creative Problem-Solving Demands and Organizational Constraints," *Journal of Creative Behavior*, 54:1, March 2020, pp. 184-195. https://onlinelibrary.wiley.com/doi/pdf/10.1002/jocb.354. Gutworth, Melissa B., and Hunter, Samual T.. "Ethical Saliency: Deterring Deviance in Creative Individuals." *Psychology of Aesthetics, Creativity, and the Arts*. Nov. 21, 2016. http://dx.doi.org/10.1037/aca0000093

9—For instance, see examples of chromesthesia at https://mymodernmet.com/synesthesia-art/ and https://www.soundoflife.com/blogs/experiences/seeing-sound-hearing-colours-exploring-the-concept-of-chromesthesia

10—Buxton, Rachel T., Pearson, Amber L., et. al. "A Synthesis of Health Benefits of Natural Sounds and Their Distribution in National Parks." *Proceedings of the National Academy of Sciences (PNAS)*. March 22, 2021. 118(14) e2013097118, https://doi.org/10.1073/pnas.2013097118

11—Beaty, Roger E., et al. "Creativity and the Default Network: A Functional Connectivity Analysis of the Creative Brain at Rest." *Neuropsychologia* vol. 64 (2014), pp. 92-98. doi:10.1016/j.neuropsychologia.2014.09.019

12—For a clear explanation of objective correlative and an example, read "What Is the Objective Correlative?" by author Ingrid Sundberg on her blog at https://ingridsnotes.wordpress.com/2013/05/14/what-is-the-objective-correlative/

Embody Summer

If spring is a spark, summer is a conflagration. Plants grow and blossom wildly, animals abound, and insects swarm busily. Summer is nature's time of frenzied growth. Although survival is less challenging than through winter and spring, this season once represented feverish labor for people, too, whether tending crops, foraging, or repairing winter damage to homes. Children were released from school because every available hand was needed, and long hours of daylight extended the workday rather than giving us more time to goof off.

Today, however, most of us don't grow our own food, so much of the labor involved has moved out of sight. Thanks in part to those school vacations, we see summer instead as a time of freedom and play. Long daylight hours and warmth bring us outdoors. We open convertible roofs and throw off clothes and shoes, revealing our bodies. Although very warm climates can discourage any activity more vigorous than napping, we move more than any other time through seasonal activities like water sports, park pickup games, and hiking. From backyards and beaches to camping and vacation travel, we stretch and explore.

Work goes on, of course, but even the pace of corporate life eases. The August slowdown in European cities is well known, while the majority of U.S. employees take allotted vacation time in July.[1] On weekends, chores lean more heavily toward yardwork, gardening, and home remodeling projects. Amid the sweat, dirt, blisters, and insect bites, there's no season in which we're more aware of our bodies and tactile sensations.

Summer energies in brief: *Rampant growth and physical development, active embodiment, passion, play, exploration, and adventure.*

Like the pain of sunburn and encounters with poison ivy, however, summer has its dark side. Summer heat ignites frenzied passions, literally and metaphorically. Summer romances may be harmless. Other passions cause trouble. The uncomfortable "dog days" of summer originated in a classical belief that when the bright Dog Star, Sirius, rises with the sun, it brings not only additional heat but fever, war, and other disasters.[2] In fact, while the star has no measurable effect on Earth's temperature, modern research validates the idea that heat increases aggression and violence.[3] Mental health issues and symptoms can be exacerbated, too.[4] And as if summer weather were not warm enough, we seem to actually celebrate short tempers and burning hearts through summer fireworks and bonfires. As a result, summer can feel like a big, hectic party that occasionally breaks into a riot.

Translating this mood into the realm of the arts brings to mind painters like Jackson Pollock flinging bright colors in all directions onto canvas. In fact, summer can be a time when creativity suffers. So many activities compete for attention! That's especially true for parents, often focused primarily on family time with kids home from school. As a result, creatives sometimes miss the chance to channel summer's frenzy of growth to develop and flesh out their projects.

The activities in this section can help—or at least keep your creativity from withering in the heat.

How to put summer energy to work

▶ **Grow and develop:** Now is the time to turn spring's ideas and tentative sprouts into robust physical form. Dig into the manual labor of shaping words, paint, fiber, or clay into something more substantial. Move nascent work—a first draft, a mostly blank canvas—substantially toward completion. In this season especially, nothing can substitute for "butt in chair" time, so rely less on the activities in this book and spend the time on your project instead. When that seems difficult or

There's no season in which we're more aware of our bodies and tactile sensations.

you feel stuck, activities such as Rely on Your Wrong Hand (p. 119), Let Your Body Inspire You (p. 101), or Ask for a Sign (p. 108) can help.

▶ **Actively embody:** Summer is all about the physical, from feeling warm sun on newly bared skin to charging down hiking trails. Activities that help you feel your work not just in your head but in your body or the physical world can be particularly useful. Get out of your chair with Shed Your Shoes (p. 99) or Let Your Body Inspire You (p. 101). Or relax while getting physical with Praise Your Hands (p. 98), Identify Your Creative Element (p. 95), or Explore Your Psychic Landscape (p. 105).

▶ **Pursue passion:** Summer burns, and your creativity should burn brightly, too. Try the activity called See Yourself as a Tree (p. 115) to assess where your fire needs fuel or gain new insights about it. Or make your project more concrete in another helpful dimension with Map Your Passion (p. 113).

▶ **Play and explore:** This season aligns with childhood in the human life cycle, so take summer's invitation to play and explore! Warm, sunny months lower the survival stakes and offer the freedom to discover something new—from a different genre or style than you usually pursue to an entirely new creative endeavor. Artists' dates have a quintessentially summer spirit, but don't just observe. Get your hands dirty. Take a class if you need the structure, or simply dive into an unfamiliar medium or activity with appropriate, inexpensive supplies or support—from paint to a local theatre's improvisation group. It'll remove the pressure you probably put on your usual creative pursuit while nurturing your creativity more broadly. In this spirit, try the Scavenger Hunt activity (p. 103), Find a Familiar (p. 111), or Create an Earth Altar (p. 117).

Take summer's invitation to play and explore.

Summer activities that follow:

Identify Your Creative Element 95
Praise Your Hands 98
Shed Your Shoes 99
Let Your Body Inspire You 101
Go on a Symbolic Thinking Scavenger Hunt 103
Explore Your Psychic Landscape 105
Ask for a Sign 108
Find a Familiar 111
Map Your Passion 113
See Yourself as a Tree 115
Create an Earth Altar 117
Rely on Your Wrong Hand 119

Identify Your Creative Element

How this can help you: Gain insight from a tangible representation of your creativity and use greater awareness of strengths to help mitigate weaknesses.

Are you burning with passion? Awash in emotion? Energized but scattered? Steady to the point of sometimes plodding?

As noted in "Fire, Water, Spikes, and Fins" in Part 1, human temperaments can be sorted by their alignment with the properties of four or five basic elements. We're using fire, water, air, and earth in this book. The characteristics of each element are broadly associated with physical, mental, psychic, and behavioral traits.[5]

Take the quiz below to determine your dominant element, which may not align with your dominant seasonal style from Part 1. For instance, I'm a hardworking winter personality whose creativity nonetheless tends toward the kookiness of air and the intensity of fire. There are advantages and disadvantages to such a mismatch. I work hard in fierce bursts and then sink back to embers for a while to recoup, and that's fine. But my airy imagination sometimes leads projects astray, or I doggedly overwork one to the point of quenching its spark. Learning to harness the element—rather than being at its mercy—is the goal.

Why this activity fits summer: *It draws on summer associations with physical embodiment and tangible sensations.*

Consider this activity a way to play with a concept that might yield insights into your work style. It can suggest approaches to optimizing your strengths while more consciously addressing any drawbacks.

Identify Your Creative Element—Step by Step

You'll need: A journal, a pen, and about 15 minutes.

1. **Select the best answer for each question** on the next two pages.
2. **Add up how many selections you picked in each column.** The column with the most is your creative element type. No clear winner? Congratulations! Balance is probably healthier, just not very common.

Wildly Inspired

My astrological birth sign is:	☐ Aries, Leo, Sagittarius	☐ Gemini, Libra, Aquarius	☐ Cancer, Scorpio, Pisces	☐ Taurus, Virgo, Capricorn
The trait that best describes me as a creator is:	☐ Energetic	☐ Thoughtful	☐ Empathic	☐ Reliable
I'm most delighted by:	☐ Deserts or lightning	☐ Cloudscapes & sunrises	☐ Ocean surf	☐ Snow-capped peaks
My worst nightmares might (or do) include:	☐ Fire	☐ Hurricane or tornado	☐ Flooding	☐ Earthquake
The most common praise from others for my creative work is that it's:	☐ Imaginative or inspiring	☐ Fun, clever, enjoyable	☐ Expressive or emotionally evocative	☐ Authentic or arresting
As a young child, my creativity began emerging mostly as:	☐ Scribbling on surfaces I shouldn't	☐ Talking, singing, or musical instruments	☐ Fingerpainting or playing in mud or with food	☐ Play-Doh, crafts, or dress-up
An art I enjoyed as a child (possibly only until teased or told I was no good):	☐ Drawing or paint-by-numbers	☐ Singing or telling jokes	☐ Cooking, makeup	☐ Dancing, fashion, or woodworking
My creative work today is, or is most like:	☐ Poetry	☐ Storytelling or theatre	☐ Journaling or music	☐ Nonfiction, sculpture, crafts
My art tends to be best when:	☐ I'm having fun with it	☐ I forget about rules	☐ It helps me understand life or myself	☐ I have a deadline
But I suspect (or critics tell me) my creative work is sometimes too:	☐ Edgy	☐ Slight or fluffy	☐ Angst-filled or self-indulgent	☐ Predictable or heavy
When faced with criticism or a setback, I might initially feel:	☐ Defensive or annoyed	☐ Dubious or dismissive	☐ Discouraged	☐ Resistant
But once I've had time to recover and consider, I'm usually:	☐ Enthusiastic about new possibilities	☐ Optimistic I can improve it	☐ Grateful for the insight	☐ Determined to get it right
When I'm not creating, I'd rather:	☐ Invent something	☐ Explore somewhere	☐ Comfort someone who needs it	☐ Lead change
When faced with change, I'm usually:	☐ Eager	☐ Uncertain	☐ Flexible	☐ Confident
When others get frustrated with me, it's often because I can be:	☐ Impulsive or selfish	☐ Flaky or forgetful	☐ Moody or dramatic	☐ Rigid or stubborn
Traits I most value in others:	☐ Passionate & inspirational	☐ Smart & independent	☐ Caring & sensitive	☐ Loyal & strong
Total the number you circled in each column:				

In addition to Artist, the archetype (of these) I am or would like to be:	☐ Rebel	☐ Explorer	☐ Magician	☐ Scholar
When it comes to my creative work, I most often work:	☐ Obsessively on one hot project	☐ On multiple projects at once	☐ When I feel like it, going with the flow	☐ On a disciplined schedule
Speaking of deadlines:	☐ I'll have it done before then	☐ Even the idea makes me tense	☐ Flexible ones are okay	☐ They help. I love them
Of the deadly sins, I'm most prone to:	☐ Wrath	☐ Pride	☐ Envy	☐ Sloth
If I'm ever imprisoned, it'll probably be for a crime of:	☐ Revenge	☐ White-collar crime	☐ Passion	☐ Need
When it comes to new stuff or ideas, I:	☐ Become an early adopter	☐ Investigate	☐ Wait and see	☐ Keep what already works for me
After a decision, I sometimes realize I should have:	☐ Considered for longer	☐ Done more research	☐ Sought more opinions	☐ Made it sooner
If I have to choose, my definition of success for my creative work is:	☐ Popularity	☐ Critical acclaim	☐ It changes someone's life	☐ It makes good money
Subtotals from this page:				
Subtotals from previous page				
Grand totals:				
	Fire	Air	Water	Earth

3. Now that you've identified your dominant element, **consider or journal on the questions** that follow.
    - What are your personal associations or experiences with your dominant element?
    - How could you bring that element more overtly into your work (images, materials, etc.)?
    - How could you bring this element more overtly into your creative practice? *(For example, by lighting a candle, taking deep breaths, playing the sounds of water in the background, or handling a favorite smooth stone, respectively.)*
    - How could you balance your creativity by incorporating more of the opposing element? (Fire balances water and air balances earth.)

Praise Your Hands

 *How this can help you:* Positive emotions like gratitude enhance creative problem solving[6] as well as reduce stress and improve overall happiness and mental health.

There's a Jewish ritual and blessing known as known as *netilat yadayim* for washing the hands after sleep. It's an act of gratitude and a reminder to use them well during the day to come. The activity that follows, inspired by this idea, shows gratitude to your hands (or your sense of the Divine) and delivers a motivational nudge to use them each day to create. This ritual is particularly meaningful for visual artists and writers, whose hands are a key channel for our creations.

Why this activity fits summer: It draws on summer's associations with our physical bodies.

Praise Your Hands—Step by Step

You'll need: Paper, colored pens or pencils, and 20–40 minutes.

1. **Trace an outline of your own hand** on a blank page. (Even if you use a prosthesis.)
2. Alongside or on the back of your drawing, **list 10 things you appreciate about your hands** and their role in your creative work. Think figuratively as well as literally.
3. Choose the five items you like best and **write one on each digit** you've drawn—or in five other locations around your drawing. See the example below.
4. **Use those five lines to create your own poem, mantra, or blessing** of appreciation. Add, subtract, or rearrange words as you like. Write the poem on the palm of your drawing or elsewhere on the page.
5. **Post or tape the result** near a sink in your kitchen or bathroom.
6. **Recite your words of gratitude whenever you wash your hands**. Notice how this gratitude affects your awareness and treatment of your hands over time, particularly when you start a creative work session.

Tickle keys, velvet, the dog;
Collect treasure, scratch every itch;
Hold life and all my beloveds.

Shed Your Shoes

How this can help you: Refreshing your awareness of non-visual sensations can equip you to bring more detail and dimensionality, and therefore authenticity, to your work.

One wet day in the woods, I took off my shoes and was startled by how much I'd been missing: The moisture in the soil, which squelched out from under my soles as it sometimes does on a wet beach. The velvety softness of dirt and the lengths of individual pine needles against my skin. Most surprising of all, how my shifting weight moved the leaves and soil beneath me.

With each step we take, our lives change, if perhaps in small ways—a new thought arises, we spy a new view, we draw closer to a goal. And as a walking companion once pointed out, each step changes the Earth, too: crushing a leaf, squishing an ant, helping a seed sprout by cracking open its hull. That barefoot day in the woods, I could feel the imprints my feet were leaving, the subtle rearrangement of humus and dirt, even when I couldn't see any trace. Then, with my boots on once more, I was surprised to still feel not only a damp graininess inside my socks but individual rocks and shifting dirt under my tread. We rarely attend just one step at a time, but that doesn't mean each doesn't echo. Thus Buddhist monk Thich Nhat Hanh's suggestion to "Walk as if you are kissing the Earth with your feet."[7]

Why this activity fits summer: *It draws on summer's associations with our physical bodies, tactile sensations, and childlike play.*

This activity asks you to feel that kiss and listen for those echoes. Most of us rarely revisit the childhood sensation of bare feet on earth, and our modern dependence on vision increasingly blinds us to other sensations. But affecting art demands a full sensory palette. Fortunately, we can "reboot" our senses with this activity.

Shed Your Shoes—Step by Step

You'll need: An audio recording device like your phone, a journal, a pen, and 10–30 minutes.

1. **With your audio recorder in hand, take off your shoes** and socks somewhere unpaved, such as in a meadow, garden, or on the edge (or middle!) of a stream. (If you have mobility issues, contact nature with other parts of your body, such as a cheek and arms on a tree.)
2. **Move in various ways for at least 2 minutes and record a running description** of what you sense or otherwise notice, such as, "Ouch, that hurt, and look out for that bee, but the grass feels silky and I hear it crinkle."

3. **Note aloud what memories or emotions surface** as a result of these sensations.
4. Sit and **write or record your answers to these questions**, preferably while your feet are still free. Refer to your recording to make sure you're not already forgetting sensations.
   - What could you feel that footwear (or other clothing) normally blocks?
   - How did your gait or thought processes change? Were your footsteps more cautious or curious?
   - What other details or associations can you excavate from memories or emotions that arose?
5. **Put your socks and shoes back on and walk again. Notice what what's changed** in your sensations, pace, foot placement, or gait. Do your steps become more determined or defiant, or are there aspects of being barefoot that remain with you?
6. Freshly attuned to your feet, **try the next activity to link sensation and imagination.** Or consider how to otherwise bring this experience to your work. For instance, how could pinched toes, aching feet, or shoes with some secret become part of an image or influence a scene, conflict, or event?

Let Your Body Inspire You

How this can help you: Embodying creative impulses or aspects of our art can surface hidden bodily knowledge to ease, speed, and enrich creative work.

Have you ever peeked at people making faces while they work at laptops? Or maybe you've been that writer, twisting your features to better grasp an emotion in words. Our bodies are wise. They learn, hold, and can reveal awareness from beyond our conscious minds—and that includes insight about your creativity, story, subject, or theme.[8] Bringing that knowledge to the surface, making the body a full participant in the creative process, can enrich, authenticate, and speed creative work. This activity is a good follow-up to Shed Your Shoes, fun with a group, or inspiring on its own when getting outside is impractical.

Why this activity fits summer: *It draws on summer's associations with our physical bodies, tactile sensations, and play.*

Let Your Body Inspire You—Step by Step

You'll need: A journal, a pen, 10-30 minutes, and space to move.

1. **Imagine footwear** that might relate to your current project. These glass slippers, high-tops, skates, or a new footwear invention might belong to a character you're working with, an artist you'd like to emulate, or your ideal audience member, for instance.

2. **Imagine the backstory of this footwear.** Are they from the past, present, or future? How did they come to your character—or to you? What dreams, memories, disappointments, events, relationships, previous owners, or makers are associated with them?

3. In the spirit of dress-up, **put on that imaginary footwear. Walk, dance, or otherwise move** in them for at least 2 minutes in the playful equivalent of "walking a mile" in someone else's shoes. Notice how your movements are encouraged, limited, or shaped. Particularly notice thoughts, emotions, or ideas they spark—including whether the shoes feel wrong for how you, in character, want to move.

4. **Answer the following questions** in your journal:
   - What did you choose, and how do they relate to your project?
   - What did putting them on make you or the character—or the shoes—feel, understand, remember, or dream?
   - What else might you or your character want to do with the footwear? *(For example, kick it off as outdated, swap for something that fits better, show them off.)*
   - What else might be found in the closet, box, or store this footwear came from? *(This might range from a different pair of foot gear to a secret.)*

Wildly Inspired

- What was your bodily reaction to this activity, and why? *(For instance, if you're self-conscious even when alone, what does that say about your attitudes toward or investment in your own creativity?)* How might you use that insight?

5. If you like, **repeat this activity with headgear** (from a soldier's helmet to a mohawk) or **an article of other clothing** appropriate to your project.
6. Pick one of the three (footwear, headgear, or clothing) and **create**—a scene, sketch, or other work—based on your explorations.

Go on a Symbolic Thinking Scavenger Hunt

How this can help you: Practice lateral and analogous thinking and expand your ability to create and communicate meaning by converting abstract ideas into tangible images.

As a kid, I was a champion Easter egg hunter and pocketer of lost coins, and I still like to find small treasures in nature—including insights for my work. This finding activity draws on a well-known creativity technique known variously as lateral, sideways, or "out of the box" thinking, which relies on surprise and funny, provocative, or even random associations.[9] It's a riff on the spring Find a Talisman activity with more practical, immediate application to a specific project. Try it as a warm-up before the (possibly more challenging) activity called Ask for a Sign, or as fun creativity play with a group.

Why this activity fits summer: *Although symbolism is associated with spring, summer is the season for converting symbolic potential to objects and action.*

Symbolic Thinking Scavenger Hunt—Step by Step

You'll need: 20–30 minutes, your phone's camera, and a journal. Pockets or a bag are optional.

1. First, **review the scavenge items below and choose four or five that most interest you**. The more abstract or creativity-oriented items can be challenging but rewarding to work with.

   Creativity-oriented things to hunt
   - ☐ Your identity as a creative
   - ☐ Art's role in your life
   - ☐ Why you create (or for whom)
   - ☐ Your satisfaction with your creative life
   - ☐ A skill you'd like to sharpen
   - ☐ Your relationship with other creatives
   - ☐ Your biggest ongoing creative challenge
   - ☐ What you need most to grow
   - ☐ Other:

   Project-oriented things to hunt
   - ☐ Your main character
   - ☐ Their biggest problem
   - ☐ What inspired this project
   - ☐ The setting
   - ☐ The antagonist
   - ☐ The mood or theme
   - ☐ A key symbol
   - ☐ A challenge you're facing with it now
   - ☐ Other:

2. **For each selected item, find something in the natural environment that seems to represent it**. Don't worry if the choice seems illogical at first. Collect smaller things as you like, but take photos or make notes about living or privately owned things you can't pick up. It's the rationale for your choice that's important.

Wildly Inspired

3. For each item you found, **answer the following questions** in your journal:
    - Why that object? How does it relate to the thing it stands for? *(For instance, one workshop participant found a fallen maple leaf to represent her main character because its parched dryness and spots of mildew represented the character's suffering and what needed to change in her life.)*
    - How does it *not* relate? List the differences. *(For instance, a character—or your artistic identity—might be a mountain standing alone… but she's not super old, nobody climbs her.)*
    - Are you sure? Are there any ways thinking about those differences might reveal an insight? *(Maybe people do "climb all over" you or your character, metaphorically, or perhaps she erupts like a volcano?)*
    - How might you incorporate anything of the symbol into your project? This might be as subtle as colors, names, or descriptives. *(Maybe the mountain character is tall or has nearly white hair).* Try it, such as by creating a test scene or sketch.
    - Now that you're thinking this way, is there a *better* symbol for that item? You needn't be restricted to something in your surroundings.
    - Finally, for any item you chose to represent a challenge, what can overcome the real object, and how could you use that idea to address your challenge? *(Say you chose a thistle because the project feels painful. Things that could overcome a thistle include being stomped on by a boot—that is, firmly take the next step—or a drenching rain that makes the prickles limp—go ahead and cry. Also note that prickles are defenses! What defenses of your own or the project's could use examination?)*

Explore Your Psychic Landscape

How this can help you: Assessing a character (or yourself) through the perspective of landscape features can help you make more conscious decisions in your work or life.

There's no landscape I enjoy more than a desert. The ocean comes in a close second, and I love them both for the same reason—they're empty. Spacious. Often silent (or at least flattened with the white noise of waves). All that space seems to flow inside me, giving my thoughts room to stretch and my heart to fly.

People have different responses to landscapes, however. I live in deep woods and experience them as embracing, even comforting—but I've known others who feel oppressed in the forest. One explained she did not feel safe anywhere but a meadow, where nothing could readily sneak up on her. Familiarity and early experience no doubt play a role.

Why this activity fits summer: *It draws on summer's associations with the physical world and the body.*

Nonetheless, most people have predictable psychological associations with specific aspects of landscape.[10] For instance, mountain peaks are a symbol of challenge, achievement, and isolation that's well recognized. Forests hold secrets. Deserts mean hardships to be endured. Such associations come into play everywhere from corporate logos to storytelling.

This activity explores such associations, opening a window into your creative psyche to reveal feelings and concerns you may be only dimly aware of so that you can more consciously address them and better reach your goals. It's also a fun approach to character development that you can use to strengthen the resonance between the character and your story's settings.

Explore Your Psychic Landscape—Step by Step

You'll need: A piece of drawing paper at least 11"x 14" in size; colored pencils, pens, or crayons; a journal; and at least 20 minutes.

1. **Draw a large outline of your body facing forward,** or find one online to print or copy. (Or draw the body of a character you're working with.) Anatomical correctness isn't important, but be sure to include recognizable areas for head, chest, belly, hands and arms, and feet and legs, at minimum. Ears, eyes, mouth, and hair are useful additions.
2. **Look over these possible landscape features** to load some possibilities in your mind:

- + Mountains, peaks, cliffs, hills
- + Meadows, grasses, flowers
- + Rivers, lakes, ocean waves, waterfalls
- + Forests, jungles, vines
- + Cactus, sand dunes, tumbleweeds
- + Paths or roads
- + Buildings or vehicles
- + Brush, shrubbery, trees
- + Sun, lightning, rain, swirling winds
- + Swamps, quicksands, whirlpools, pits
- + Caves, ditches, earthquake cracks

3. **Fill in the outline by drawing different landscape, weather, or nature images** (symbols or stick figures are fine) in various parts of the body and head. Follow your intuition for what goes where. Color can help you distinguish various features, and elements can be positioned outside of the body as well (such as a crown of flowers around the top of the head).

4. When the body outline feels filled enough, **refer to these common psychological associations with landscape features**. Note that contradictions are common, but your heart will know which interpretation holds more meaning for you. Sometimes disagreeing with an interpretation points most clearly to a better meaning for you.

    + Mountains: Ambition, goals (achievable or distant), difficulty or risks, focus, isolation, uphill battles or turbulence, achievement after hard work, long-term perspective, superiority
    + Rivers, waterfalls, other waters: Vitality, communication, direction, irresistible forces or lack of control, risk, danger of eddies or stagnancy
    + Meadows, grasses, flowers: Openness, thriving, optimism, growth
    + Brush, forests, jungles, shrubbery, etc.: Complexity, confusion, blockages, obstacles, danger, hidden information, or interconnectedness, vitality, and the security of being unseen
    + Trees: Standing alone or with others, shelter, rootedness, immobility, fruitfulness
    + Swamps, oceans: Danger, stagnation, instability, entrapment, but also fecundity, mystery, opportunity
    + Desert, cactus: Thirst, aridity, isolation, feeling lost or in hostile territory, but also freedom, silence, resilience
    + Paths or roads: Guidance, plans, movement or direction, inevitability
    + Caves, ravines: Depths, mysteries, but also refuge
    + Buildings: Comfort, sense of companionship or protection, assistance, security
    + Weather: Pretty intuitive (storms evoke conflict, for instance), but opposites are really common for this particular category, such as sun standing either for happiness and optimism or a "fixed smile" sort of oppression; winds may suggest energy and motility or confusion and resistance, lightning is vitality and inspiration or threat, clouds may be a gloomy outlook or a fluffy, lightness of spirit, etc.
    + Other nature images: Your own instincts regarding subtle meanings will be your best guidance for any other images you included, from animals or other people to rainbows or UFOs.

5. Referring to the symbolism suggested but following your own instincts more, **answer these questions for yourself in a journal**:
    - What did you put in or around the head? How might that reflect the state of thoughts, anxieties, confusion, or knowledge?
    - Is anything in particular associated with the eyes (perception, insight), ears (hearing, connection to the outside world), or mouth (communication, nourishment) whose symbolism seems significant?
    - What fills or surrounds the feet and lower legs, and how might that relate to a sense of stability, grounding in reality, or ability to move forward?
    - What fills or surrounds the upper legs, hips, and/or back, and how might that relate to the sense of feeling supported, and by what?
    - What's in the area of the heart, and how might that relate to the state of your (or the character's) passion, courage, or fears?
    - What's in the lower abdomen, and how might that relate to determination, persistence, hunger, or other desires?
    - What's in your hands and arms, and how might that relate to a sense of agency, capability, or abundance?
    - What area of the body, given the images you put there, feels most energetic? What areas feel hollow, tangled, or constrained?
    - How are any of the images that seem most important, or the ideas and feelings associated with them, serving you (or the character)? How might their associations be a hindrance?
6. **Identify one image, in one part of the body, that seems problematic** and that you (or the character) might like to change. What landscape feature might be more ideal instead? What steps could you take that might help you make the transition from one to the other?

    For instance, post an image of the sort of landscape feature you'd like to move toward, or spend some time Googling or journaling about such a landscape, considering why it appeals and imagining how to better access those traits.

Ask for a Sign

How this can help you: Practice converting abstract thinking into physical objects and encourage subconscious answers to creative problems to rise into consciousness.

Most artists struggle with creative decisions or problems. It can feel as though the harder you think about it, the more elusive an answer becomes—and that's probably true, because creative solutions often require a period of "incubation" when we're not consciously working on them.[11] That's why we have clichés about ideas striking during a hot shower. But you don't have to wait passively for a solution from the showerhead.

Why this activity fits summer: *It draws on summer's associations with the earth element and physical embodiment, including ideas manifested in physical form.*

Engaging in mostly mindless motion invokes the creative state characterized by theta brainwaves, which can heat up that subconscious incubation and jostle free insights.

My most dramatic example came once while I was running and pondering a problem in my current project. I turned a familiar corner and confronted a worn snatch of graffiti I'd never noticed before. It read, "You already know what to do."

With a mental shock, I realized that was true. As the odd message said, I knew how to fix the problem—I was just reluctant to face the amount of work involved. But I had my answer, ran home, and got started.

You needn't believe in a divinity that sends signs in spray paint. What you notice around you—or not—is dramatically influenced by your brain, which filters out the majority of the sensory information bombarding us as irrelevant to our most pressing concerns.[12] Can you hear your own pulse or feel the texture of the inside of your clothes? Your senses constantly collect that information; your brain is just choosing not to notify you. This filtering is responsible for phenomena such as not noticing many, say, Volkswagens on the road until you buy one. Suddenly, they seem to be everywhere.

There's no change in the Volkswagen volume. Rather, your brain has declared Volkswagens newly relevant and allowed information about them to slip through.

While our filters are useful, they tend to suppress innovation. This activity can help reset an overprotective filter and allow creative insights through. I think of this more advanced, purposeful version of the Symbolic Thinking Scavenger Hunt as asking the universe for a sign.

Ask for a Sign—Step by Step

You'll need: 20–40 minutes and something easy to carry with which to take notes, such as your phone notes or a voice recording app.

1. **Change your surroundings.** Leave your usual creative workspace and head out into nature, from a local park to your own backyard.
2. **Engage your body in low-demand movement.** Walking or weeding are good examples—anything that doesn't take too much focus or keep you stuck in one place.
3. **Hold your question or creative challenge uppermost in your mind.** When your attention wanders, reclaim it. In some ways, this is the opposite of meditation (another good way to solicit a sign, but one many people find challenging).
4. **Look around, down, into corners and shadows.** What do you notice? Focus on images, your emotional responses to them, and what appear to be random, unprovoked thoughts. Look especially for the unexpected or, if you're anywhere familiar, things you haven't noticed before, such as an unusual bird, out-of-place plant, or startling litter.
5. Also **consider a more useful question: What *don't* you notice?** If you tend to watch your path, you may be missing answers at eye-level or above. Or behind you. Or you may be suddenly aware of an absence that might hold your answer.
6. **When something strikes you, consider how you could interpret it**—no matter how wildly—as applying to the issue you're struggling with. Consider as many meanings as you can, even if it feels like you're inventing them. You are! Some examples:
    + A knot of roots might confirm you have a mess, suggest you untangle it by focusing on one strand at a time, or perhaps tell you to look closer at the root of the problem.
    + A gleaming reflection of the sky in a puddle suggests the trouble is not as murky as you think or tells you to look for a silver lining—or perhaps in the opposite direction, up instead of down.
    + A candy bar wrapper could imply you're trying too hard to be sweet or need to properly dispose of something in the work.
    + If eerie silence, free of bird or insect sounds, reminds you that you're alone, perhaps you need to seek help from a comrade, explore what others have done in the same situation, or turn onto a new path.

    If nothing strikes you, note key images anyway. Sometimes "signs" encountered in one frame of mind take on new meaning later. Google may help.

    For example, you may notice a snake without knowing that snakes are symbols of transformation and growth, thanks to their habit of shedding their skin. The snake was not there for your benefit, of course. But you noticed—when you may regularly pass by this easily camouflaged creature. That suggests your subconscious might find a snake particularly relevant now. Your mind may be trying to tell you something in its primary language—imagery. If so, you'd be wise to heed it.

7. When you hit an interpretation that resonates with your heart, you'll know it's the answer from within. **Act accordingly.** The more you practice and honor this kind of intuitive insight, the more easily it will come.

Find a Familiar

How this can help you: Gain a symbolic confidant and companion who can inspire and subtly support your creativity.

In European lore, witches welcomed familiars—animal companions with supernatural powers who could help them with their work.

As a caster of spells through writing, I have a familiar, too, though it took me a while to recognize it. I once owned a horse named Jack who was as friendly as an oversized dog, if sometimes too frisky to be easy to handle. Early in my writing career, I began having two recurring nightmares about him.

In the first, I'd forgotten to feed him for some unknown time. In the other, I was riding him along an awkward height—a razor-thin ridge, a staircase, the roof of a building—with no idea how to get us safely down. I began dreading reruns of both anxious dreams.

Finally, my subconscious sent me a hint. In a new dream, someone at the barn kept calling my horse "Art." Annoyed, I informed them, "His name isn't Art. It's Jack."

When I woke, I laughed, finally getting the homophonic convergence of "riding" and "writing." Jack had become a symbol for my writing, my art—great fun but occasionally out of my control. The starving horse dream told me I needed to feed my creativity more, that it'd been too long since I'd written or enjoyed artsy play. The other nightmare's meaning was now obvious, too. When you aren't sure how to guide your horse through tricky terrain, you release the reins and let him choose, trusting his instincts to get you both to safety. I needed to do the same for whatever novel I was struggling with—stop trying to control it and trust the story to find its way home.

Why this activity fits summer: *Like plant life, animals tend to be more active and visible in summer, which is associated with physical manifestations, including those of character traits.*

These days, the real Jack grazes in horse heaven, but he still appears in my dreams as my writing familiar. He reminds me that working with a horse—or a story—requires sensitivity, trust, and a partnership based on requests, not demands. Besides, who knows more than a horse about taking people on journeys into new territories, bucking off predators, and galloping forward with strength, endurance, and heart? When he visits, I take his advice.

You don't have to wait for a meaningful dream. You can choose an animal familiar based on traits you'd like to embrace or that can help you perform creative magic. If you're lucky, your subconscious will begin working with the image of that creative companion—and the *animi mundi* may even surprise you with in-person sightings.

Find a Familiar—Step by Step

You'll need: Only a journal, some imagination, and 15 minutes. More time, an Internet connection for research, and origami or other craft supplies are optional.

1. In a journal, **list half a dozen creatures you're drawn to.** This might include animals that arise in the Rely on Your Wrong Hand activity that comes later.

2. For each, **note a few of their real, observed, or culturally assigned traits** that you might like to bring to bear on your work. Fairy tales and Disney movies are a good source of stereotypical associations, from the hardworking ant to the beleaguered donkey.

3. **List another half-dozen**, adding more unusual creatures and traits. We all can appreciate wise owls, clever foxes, and playful dolphins, but creatures with more unique associations might be more meaningful for you. *For instance, a woodpecker keeps pounding until it reaches its objectives, and its work is known far and wide through the forest.*

4. **Select one of the creatures from your list and answer the following questions about it:**
   - What does your familiar eat? Since it's a supernatural creature, this menu needn't align with nature. Play with images and metaphors to come up with a "food" that supports your symbiotic relationship. *For instance, the woodpecker might eagerly gobble the worms of self-doubt that bore into your confidence.*
   - What environments does your familiar favor? How can you relate those places to your work, whether by imagination or analogy?
   - How social or independent is your familiar, and how can you draw on those traits for yourself? For instance, an ant or bee might encourage you to have more fun networking, sit invisibly on your shoulder to boost your confidence when you do, even prompt you to try collaborating. On the other hand, a hummingbird might jealously and noisily guard the territory your work should have on your schedule.
   - How else could your familiar help you in your work? Perhaps your woodpecker drills into mundane topics and plucks out strands of color for you to work into your art. Or maybe it flies high to bring you reports of a broader perspective.

5. When you feel you know your familiar, **invite it into your workspace** with a photo or drawing, a clay or origami model, a physical token of it such as a feather, or a toy version. (An Internet search will turn up lots of free origami instructions for a wide range of creatures.)

6. **Give your familiar a name. Ask it for help when you need it**.

7. **Finally, keep an eye out for your familiar**. Even if the real creature lives nowhere near your community, you might be surprised by an increase in how often you notice it in media. Now that you've made it important, it may sneak past the relevance filter in your brain more often. Let each sighting remind you of the power of your imagination, and get to work on your art!

Map Your Passion

How this can help you: Engage more of your brain in your creative pursuit and make your creative journey more tangible to reveal options and keep your art moving ahead.

In today's world of apps, paper maps are nearly obsolete. They're probably used more often in collages or for wrapping gifts than for navigating. But there are advantages to the tangible, big-picture perspective of a paper map—and creating your own can be revealing, inspiring, and fun. That's particularly true when the territory on the map is not a location at all but a mental position, a narrative, or a process.

First, map-making (like many of the activities in this book) offers practice in connecting the material world with a symbolic one. Doing so can make the abstract concept of a project or creative journey easier to grasp while revealing options and paths otherwise overlooked.

Why this activity fits summer: *It draws on summer's associations with the physical and exploration.*

In addition, for creators such as writers whose art doesn't typically involve drawing or painting, this visual activity engages a different part of the brain. It works in a way similar to mind mapping—which is strongly associated with greater creativity[13]—in that it can reveal connections, increase mental flexibility, suggest alternate structures or perspectives, and illuminate pitfalls.

Finally, associating features from your physical surroundings with your artistic landscape can turn those geographical features into a prompt. If a bridge you cross daily also represents a connection you'd like to make in your creative work, for instance, that repeated reminder can nudge you to prioritize and achieve that goal.

Map Your Passion—Step by Step

You'll need: Drawing supplies such as colored pens or pencils, 45–60 minutes, a journal, and a blank paper or, if you like, a printed local map you can ruin.

1. **Pick a shape that's meaningful to your current project** or your creative passion in general. It might be a symbol from your work or a part of your body you associate with your creativity, such as a hand, a heart, or an eye.
2. **Draw or trace the shape** on your paper or a printed map you'll use as a background. Accuracy isn't important. Work larger rather than smaller.
3. **Consider the shape on your paper as though you're studying a satellite image or road map.** Using all your senses, including imagination, notice or impose heights and

lowlands, potential water courses, and other kinds of terrain. The area might be wild or urban, compact or immense. Think symbolically and intuitively.

4. Next, **draw five to eight notable features of the actual landscape around you onto your map**. Choose features using whatever scale you like—from mountain ranges and rivers to your garden's seedbeds and watering hose. Or, if you used a printed map as your paper, highlight or elaborate on key features from it. Add details, icons, or labels as needed. Play.

5. Now **imagine your creative career or a specific project as territory that you (or the project's protagonist) are traveling through**. You (or your character) are somewhere in the middle of Passion Land now. Mark that spot with a star.

6. **Consider how you (or your character) got to this point** on the journey, and from which direction on your map. Trace a trail or road to where you (or they) are now. Add or annotate features along the way for past challenges (a dead end or a pile of dog poop?) and past successes (a crossroads or a viewpoint?).

7. **Add the following to your map**:
    - What landmarks are in the vicinity now? Perhaps there's a place for family, a day job, hobbies—or various styles, creative pursuits, or genres. Draw or label them.
    - Decide which way you're traveling next: south to north, west to east, zigzagging all over, or perhaps in a spiral. Do you have a destination, do you need a change in direction, or are you simply exploring? How can you reflect any of these on your map?
    - Invent icons for skills, mentors, or treasures you or your character have found—or need to find. Add them to your map, with labels as needed.
    - Map a route forward with arrows or a dotted line. Consider what challenges lie ahead on that route. Should you add bridges, detours, or shortcuts?
    - Don't worry if your map gets messy. Creativity is messy. Just highlight or emphasize what's most important.

8. When your map feels robust, sit back and **answer the questions below** in a journal.
    - What surprises or realizations appear for you? (For instance, when I did one version of this map, I was struck by how much the path forward I'd drawn diverged from the road I'd included. I think that indicates I'm subconsciously expecting to forge my own way.)
    - What aspects of your map don't you like, find troublesome, or would like to do over? What concerns might these represent about your creative path? How would you or could you change them?
    - If a friend asked you to explain your map, what would you say? What might you keep to yourself? Why?

9. **As you interact with the real geographical features on your map, recall the connections you've built** between those features, your passion, and your path forward. Let them remind you to keep making creative progress.

10. **Post or view your map over time as a reminder** of how far you've come and of goals still ahead.

See Yourself as a Tree

How this can help you: Practice creative visualization and reveal hidden perceptions about your creative life so you can build on, address, or change them.

Trees are one of the most prominent symbols of the seasons, from winter's bare branches or evergreens to the blazing colors of fall. They're deeply embedded in the collective unconscious as broader symbols as well. Many cultures have "world trees," such as the Norse Yggdrasil, the Hindu Ashvattha, or the consequential trees in the Garden of Eden. These deep symbolic connections are probably why drawings of trees are one part of a common personality test.[14] The resulting tree and its interpretations are thought to reflect unconscious, repressed, or partly buried aspects of the personality, self-image, and social connectedness.

Why this activity fits summer: *It draws on summer's associations with the verdant Earth and physical embodiment.*

This activity uses such a drawing to probe specific aspects of your creativity, spark insights hiding in the shadows of your mind, and help you act on the results to get where you want to go. It can be fun and enlightening to do with a creative friend, comparing and discussing the results. *Storytellers:* You can work through this activity from the perspective of a character, but I recommend you do it for yourself first.

See Yourself as a Tree—Step by Step

You'll need: Colored pens or pencils, a big (e.g., 11" x 17") piece of paper, a journal, a quiet and preferably dim space to work undisturbed, an Internet connection to access the 12-minute recorded meditation at https://youtu.be/vcB2Z3Q_XDk, and 45–60 minutes.

1. **Prepare your materials and workspace.** Consider lighting a candle or working only by light shining from another room.
2. Get comfortable, **listen to the meditation** at https://youtu.be/vcB2Z3Q_XDk, and follow its instructions.
3. When you're done drawing, **turn your paper over and shift your focus.** Get a drink, move to a different location, or wait until tomorrow to do the next step.
4. With fresh eyes, **look at your drawing. Set aside any artistic judgment and answer the following questions** in your journal:
    - **Overall**: What do you notice about the size, shape, age, colors, or isolation of your tree compared with the paper or scene around it? Does its environment feel nurturing or harsh (e.g., is it alone in a city or desert)? Has your tree been singed or broken? The

answers can indicate how you feel about your creative life and mental state overall. What insights are suggested by that framing?

- **Foliage**: What do you notice about your tree's branches and leaves? Do they swoop up with ambition or droop? Are any broken, missing, or tangled? Are they abundant or skimpy? In your imagination, do they flutter or rest silent and still? How do your answers reflect how strong, balanced, or capable you feel in your skills, productivity, or creative processes?
- **Top**: What do you notice about the top of your tree? Is it reaching, floppy, rounded, broad, or sharp? Does it rise above everything, or is it surrounded by birds or clouds? The answers typically reflect your ambitions and dreams, your sense of pride or direction, or your confidence in your ability to reach your goals. How does that information resonate?
- **Surroundings**: How does your tree's community feel—peaceful, friendly, distracting, hostile? Is your tree enjoying the sun or enduring a storm? Is there a body of water, meadow, or mountain in the scene? (In psychology, mountains are associated with introversion. Open plains and the ocean are associated with extroversion, while proximity to lakes, rivers, or the sea apparently correlate with better mental health.[15] Do any of these appear in your drawing, and if so, does that information resonate for you?) How many companions did you include, and are they supportive—or nibbling on leaves? How do your answers reflect your sense of being supported, undermined, or able to connect with like-minded others?
- **Contents**: What's in your tree or among its branches, and how do you feel about holding those things in your arms? How big or numerous are fruits, flowers, or anything that might represent your creative products? How might these items in the branches represent family or other responsibilities, how much you're juggling or producing, and how well?
- **Delights**: What about your drawing gives you joy? What do you love about your tree, and why? What might this represent in your creative life and how can you get more of it?
- **Improvements**: What do you wish your tree or its surroundings had more of, or less of? Is there any wistful absence or an element you resent or fear? Consider what such elements might represent in your creative life.
- **The future**: What clues can you find or intuit about what happens next to your tree, whether in terms of seasons or weather or visitors or change?
- **Bodily reactions:** As you've studied your drawing and considered these questions, what emotions or sensations (such as heaviness or nervous energy) have arisen in your own body or skin? Does your tree amuse or sadden you or make you proud? What might these various feelings be hinting?

5. **Pick one image or idea from your drawing you'd like to change**. Focusing on things you can control, journal about what you could change in your life or creative practice to result in a subtly happier tree in six months.

6. **Write down at least three concrete steps** you'll take to make that change happen.

7. **Share your plans with a friend** or your creative community, so you'll be more likely to follow through on this commitment to your own well-being.

8. Set your drawing aside and **return to it later**. After you've done other activities in this book, you may spot recurring images or themes, or your interpretations may change. Did you keep your Step 6 commitment to yourself, or do you feel differently now?

Create an Earth Altar

How this can help you: Enhance creativity by reducing stress,[16] engaging in free play,[17] and working within constraints[18] while internalizing useful principles of aesthetics.

I've joked with relatives that when I die, they can simply toss half my possessions into the yard. That's because my windowsills, shelves, and bathroom nooks are filled with interesting rocks, dried seedpods, shells, and other fully biodegradable treasures from nature. So when I stumbled across land art practitioners such as Jon Foreman, Pascal Fiechter, Michael Grab, and Andy Goldsworthy who stack rocks in pools or arrange leaves in spirals and stars, I wanted to try it.

Of course, the effects these artists achieve are harder than they look, but it's wonderfully meditative to try using natural detritus such as twigs, pine cones, rocks, berries, and leaves. Whether you call it a mandala, sculpture, altar, or art installation, this play can hone your creativity's response to constraints and impart lessons about contrast, pattern, textures, balance, and other basic aesthetic principles. Try it on a sunny day to reduce stress while encouraging your brain's default network (see p. 64 in Spring), from which other inspirations may flow.

Why this activity fits summer: *It draws on summer's associations with physical interaction and play.*

Create an Earth Altar—Step by Step

You'll need: Your phone, whatever you can find outdoors, and 20–40 minutes. A journal and pen are optional.

1. **Find a site outdoors** where you can work without being self-conscious. Consider a sunny meadow or field, a clearing in the woods, or an inviting log on the beach.
2. **Examine what's around you within a small area** to identify the materials at your disposal. (For a greater challenge, stick to items within only a few paces or arm's reach.) Notice a variety of shapes, colors, sizes, textures, patterns.
3. **Select half a dozen elements that appeal to you.** (And possibly a few you resist—which may include intriguing litter. Humans are part of nature, for better or worse.) Stick to things that are inanimate or already dead, berries or seeds (which want to be dispersed), and growth or blossoms that are so abundant that your reaping can't be noticed.
4. **Identify or create a canvas for your work** by clearing a small space on the ground or finding a flat rock, stump or log, chunk of smooth bark, or similar background.
5. **Arrange your materials in whatever way you find pleasing.** For mandala shapes like the examples, consider a unique centerpiece and work out from there. Note that smaller designs can be more challenging than larger ones, especially if it's breezy.
6. **Explore the possibilities of your materials.** What if you split leaves in half or turn them upside down, or incorporate senses other than vision by, for instance, placing pebbles as if on a music staff to represent notes of birdsong?
7. **Play and let your mind wander**. Rearrange or remove elements that don't work. When the sculpture feels complete, take a photo. Consider sharing it on social media.
8. If you like, **answer these questions** for yourself in a journal:
   - What about your design pleases you? How does it capture your current mood or personal aesthetic? (Consider materials, shape, scale, symmetry, complexity, etc.)
   - What might you change if you tried again? How much perfectionism rose in the process?
   - How do you feel about its transience? Do similar feelings apply to or affect your other creative efforts?
   - How can you bring this experience or its lessons to your usual creative work?
9. **This activity is ideal for a regular, repeat practice**, so try it again somewhere else and with different materials. Watch how your style or creative reveries develop.

Rely on Your Wrong Hand

How this can help you: Encourage right-brain activity to integrate different areas of your brain, reach insights from the subconscious, and inspire greater creativity.

The full moon—briefly whole in its cycle of waxing and waning—makes a good metaphor for accessing our full brainpower. We shine best, too, when connecting and engaging both the logical, linguistic, task-oriented regions of our brains and those that tend to be more engaged in holistic, emotional, intuitive, and creative thinking. (It's an oversimplification to think of the two sides of our brains handling completely different functions. But there *are* regional differences, areas of specialization, and benefits to increased connectivity and balance.[19] So for those of us who are not neurologists—and in a society heavily biased toward rational, reductive, "left-brain" thinking—there's no downside to wooing the more global and meaning-oriented perspective popularly associated with the right side of the brain.) A writing and drawing technique using your nondominant hand can help. It gives voice to the less-verbal half of your brain for a mind as rounded and bright as the full moon.

Why this activity fits summer: *It draws on summer's associations with shedding light via a noon sun and using the body in movement and play.*

I have encountered this technique in a variety of contexts. Art therapists use it to access subconscious or emotional awareness,[20] while writing instructors use it to mute the internal critic. It can feel awkward, challenging, or silly. But the results often reveal surprising insights. I like to incorporate exposure to nature, which is inherently more visual and non-directed, and thus more "right-brained."

This activity can be particularly effective when done with a partner. Sharing answers and observations with another person often uncovers food for more thought.

Rely on Your Wrong Hand—Step by Step

You'll need: A journal or blank paper, writing and drawing pens or pencils, and 20–40 minutes.

1. **Writing with your dominant hand, quickly answer these questions**: If you were an animal, which one would it be? Why? (Don't think about it too hard.)
2. **Spend a few moments gazing at something complex from nature**, such as a busy ant pile, passing clouds, a forest canopy, or the yard outside your window. Try to keep your focus on the big picture (rather than individual ants or leaves).

3. **Moving your pen to your nondominant hand, ask yourself** what *other* animal you might be and why, this time **writing the answer with your nondominant hand**. Don't worry about the handwriting; no one else needs to see it.
4. **Reflect on how your two answers compare.** Dominant-hand answers typically reflect a self we present to the world or wishful thinking; answers revealed by the nondominant hand more typically reflect inner realities or suspicions. What do they have in common, if anything?
5. Now **use your nondominant hand to draw an image of your creativity or a current project**. (It may be literal, symbolic, or completely abstract—let impulse guide you.) Again, you're not going for quality art. Sticks or scribbles are fine, but don't stop until it feels complete.
6. **Answer these questions about your drawing**. Use your nondominant hand for deeper answers. You can always elaborate using your dominant hand if need be.
    - How colorful is it? What meanings or emotions do the dominant colors evoke?
    - How much space does it take on the page, and where? What are the implications for its space in your life? *(For example, near the top? Central? Expansive or compressed?)*
    - What is the drawing's overall mood or impression? How symmetrical, orderly, or messy is it? Does this resonate with your feelings about your creativity or its place in your life?
    - Are there specific shapes or symbols included—e.g., hearts, growing things, flames, boxes, prison bars, goal-oriented arrows? How might you interpret them? How does turning your image upside down or sideways change your view or impressions?
    - What adjectives would you use to describe your image? These might range from exuberant to limp. What adjectives would you prefer for describing your creativity itself?
    - Consider your drawing's lines and line weights. What do they suggest about passion (heavy lines), intricacy (small details), confusion, tentativeness, or energy levels? (Using your "wrong" hand will influence these, but consider if you're using that excuse to avoid a truth.)
    - If you were naming this image to hang it in a gallery, what would you call it? What does that name suggest about your creativity or attitudes toward it?
    - How does this drawing relate (or not) to the animals or traits you named in questions 1 or 3?
7. **Identify one insight** from this activity that might help you bring more of yourself and your subconscious into your creative practice.

Summer Endnotes

1—Saad, Lydia. "Majority of Americans Plan to Vacation This Summer." Gallup Polls, May 31, 2002. https://news.gallup.com/poll/6112/majority-americans-plan-vacation-summer.aspx

2—Little, Becky. "Here's Why We Call this Time of Year the Dog Days of Summer." *National Geographic.* July 16, 2021. https://www.nationalgeographic.com/animals/article/150710-dog-days-summer-sirius-star-astronomy-weather-language

3—Anderson, Craig A. "Heat and Violence." *Current Directions in Psychological Science.* American Psychological Society. 10:1. Feb. 1, 2001. https://doi.org/10.1111/1467-8721.00109

4—Rony, Moustaq Karim Khan and Hasnat M. Alamgir. "High Temperatures on Mental Health: Recognizing the Association and the Need for Proactive Strategies—A Perspective." *Health Science Reports* 6:12 e1729. Dec. 4, 2023. https://doi.org/10.1002/hsr2.1729

5— For example, see Harden, Jim, and Dude, Brad. *What Makes You Tick and What Ticks You Off.* Snow in Sarasota Publishing, 2009

6—Isen, A. M., et al. "Positive Affect Facilitates Creative Problem Solving." *Journal of Personality and Social Psychology* 52:6 (1987), pp. 122-31. https://doi.org/10.1037//0022-3514.52.6.1122; Emmons, Robert A., and McCullough, Michael E. "Counting Blessings Versus Burdens: An Experimental Investigation of Gratitude and Subjective Well-Being in Daily Life." *Journal of Personality and Social Psychology* 84:2 (February 2003), pp. 377-389. https://doi.org/10.1037/0022-3514.84.2.377; https://www.proquest.com/openview/5937047669ecf-c2c5524db291321052c/1; Zahn, Roland, et al. "The Neural Basis of Human Social Values: Evidence from Functional MRI." *Cerebral Cortex* 19:2 (2009), pp. 276-283. https://doi.org/10.1093/cercor/bhn080; Wong, Y. Joel, et. al. "Does Gratitude Writing Improve the Mental Health of Psychotherapy Clients? Evidence from a Randomized Controlled Trial." *Psychotherapy Research*, 28:2, pp. 192-202, https://doi.org/10.1080/10503307.2016.1169332

7—Hanh, Thich Naht. *Peace Is Every Step: The Path of Mindfulness in Everyday Life.* New York: Random House, 1992

8—van der Kolk, Bessel. *The Body Keeps the Score: Brain, Mind, and Body in the Healing of Trauma.* New York: Penguin, 2015; Claxton, Guy. *Intelligence in the Flesh.* London: Yale University Press, 2015; Freiler, Tammy J. "Learning Through the Body." *New Directions for Adult and Continuing Education*, 2008: 37-47. https://doi.org/10.1002/ace.304; Nguyen, D.J., and Larson, J.B. "Don't Forget About the Body: Exploring the Curricular Possibilities of Embodied Pedagogy." *Innovations in Higher Education* 40 (2015), pp. 331–344. https://doi.org/10.1007/s10755-015-9319-6; Gillath, Omri, et al. "Shoes as a Source of First Impressions." *Journal of Research in Personality* 46:4 (2012), pp. 423-430. https://doi.org/10.1016/j.jrp.2012.04.003

9—Beda, Zsolt, et al. "Creativity on Demand—Hacking into Creative Problem Solving," *NeuroImage* vol. 216 (2020). https://doi.org/10.1016/j.neuroimage.2020.116867

10—Appleton, Jay. *The Experience of Landscape, Rev. Ed.* Chichester: Wiley, 1996; Cosgrove, Denis and Stephen Daniels, eds. *The Iconography of Landscape*. Cambridge: Cambridge University Press, 1988. Kaplan, R. and Kaplan, S. *The Experience of Nature: A Psychological Perspective*. New York: Cambridge University Press, 1989; Roo, Benjamin. "A Three-Step Process for Mapping Your Life Change." *Better Humans*, Nov. 3, 2021. https://betterhumans.pub/a-3-step-process-for-mapping-your-life-change-abd4a8577e9b

11—Ritter, Simone M., and Dijksterhuis, Ap. "Creativity—The Unconscious Foundations of the Incubation Period." *Frontiers in Human Neuroscience*, 8:215 (2014). https://doi.org/10.3389/fnhum.2014.00215

12—This filtering, a function of the brain's salience network, is known as selective attention. It's a potential source of cognitive bias, including the Baader-Meinhof phenomenon responsible for the Volkswagen example described in the introduction to this activity. The cars' frequency hasn't changed; they've just become more salient and therefore are newly allowed into conscious awareness. Murphy, T. Franklin. "Selective Attention: A Cognitive Function." *Psychology Fanatic*. July 13, 2024. https://psychologyfanatic.com/selective-attention; Nikolopoulou, Kassiani. "The Baader-Meinhof Phenomenon Explained." *Scribbr*, Nov. 22, 2022. https://www.scribbr.com/research-bias/baader-meinhof-phenomenon; Shofty, B., et al. "The Default Network Is Causally Linked to Creative Thinking." *Molecular Psychiatry* 27 (2022), pp. 1848–1854. https://doi.org/10.1038/s41380-021-01403-8

13—Much research on mind-mapping's effects on creativity include Malycha, Charlotte P., and Maier, Günter W. "Enhancing Creativity on Different Complexity Levels by Eliciting Mental Models." *Psychology of Aesthetics, Creativity, and the Arts* 11:2 (2017), p. 187; Malycha, Charlotte P., and Maier, Günter W. "The Random-Map Technique: Enhancing Mind-Mapping with a Conceptual Combination Technique to Foster Creative Potential." *Creativity Research Journal* 29:2 (2017), pp. 114-124; Higgins, James M. "Creating Creativity." *Training & Development*, 48:11 (Nov. 1994), p. 11+. https://link.gale.com/apps/

doc/A16458874/AONE; Wang, Wen-Cheng, et al. "A Brief Review on Developing Creative Thinking in Young Children by Mind Mapping." *International Business Research*, 3:3 (July 2010). https://pdfs.semanticscholar.org/c6a5/c65363c2823ee56215636cc35c229f4d2318.pdf

14—https://www.encyclopedia.com/medicine/encyclopedias-almanacs-transcripts-and-maps/house-tree-person-test

15—Considerable research on these points includes Oishi, Shigehiro et al. "Personality and Geography: Introverts Prefer Mountains." *Journal of Research in Personality*, Vol. 58 (2015), pp. 55-68. https://doi.org/10.1016/j.jrp.2015.07.001; William J. Chopik and Motyl, Matt. "Is Virginia for Lovers? Geographic Variation in Adult Attachment Orientation." *Journal of Research in Personality*, Vol. 66 (2017), pp. 8-45. https://doi.org/10.1016/j.jrp.2016.12.004; De Bell, Siân, et al. "The Importance of Nature in Mediating Social and Psychological Benefits Associated with Visits to Freshwater Blue Space." *Landscape and Urban Planning* 167 (2017), pp. 118-127; Gascon, Mireia, et al. "Outdoor Blue Spaces, Human Health, and Well-Being: A Systematic Review of Quantitative Studies." *International Journal of Hygiene and Environmental Health* 220.8 (2017), pp. 1207-1221; Dzhambov, Angel M., et al. "Multiple Pathways Link Urban Green-and Bluespace to Mental Health in Young Adults." *Environmental Research* 166 (2018): pp. 223-233; De Vries, Sjerp, et al. "Local Availability of Green and Blue Space and Prevalence of Common Mental Disorders in the Netherlands." *British Journal of Psychology—Open*, 2.6 (2016), pp. 366-372; White, M. P., et al. "Coastal Proximity and Health: A Fixed Effects Analysis of Longitudinal Panel Data." *Health Place* 23 (2013), pp. 97-103; Pasanen, Tytti P., et al. "Neighbourhood Blue Space, Health and Wellbeing: The Mediating Role of Different Types of Physical Activity." *Environment International* 131 (2019). https://doi.org/10.1016/j.envint.2019.105016

16—Vartanian, Oshin, et al. "The Creative Brain Under Stress: Considerations for Performance in Extreme Environments," *Frontiers in Psychology* vol. 11, Oct. 29, 2020. https://doi.org/10.3389/fpsyg.2020.585969

17—Bateson, Patrick & Martin, Paul. *Play, Playfulness, Creativity and Innovation.* Cambridge: Cambridge University Press, 2013

18—Stokes, Patricia D. *Creativity from Constraints: The Psychology of Breakthrough.* New York: Springer, 2005

19—McCrea, Simon M. "Intuition, Insight, and the Right Hemisphere: Emergence of Higher Sociocognitive Functions." *Psychology

Research and Behavior Management vol. 3 (2010), pp. 1-39. https://doi.org/10.2147/prbm.s7935; McGilchrist, Iain. *The Master and His Emissary: The Divided Brain and the Making of the Western World*. London: Yale University Press, 2009

20—Gupta, Sharat. "Doodling: The Artistry of the Roving Metaphysical Mind." *Journal of Mental Health and Human Behaviour* 21:1 (Jan.-June 2016), pp. 16-19. https://doi.org/10.4103/0971-8990.182097

Fall Inward

The fall season is like aerial fireworks: It bursts and then fades. Energy explodes with a new school year or a more grown-up commitment to get "back to work" after summer delights and vacations. Within weeks, that thrill sags to more of a grind. Depending on the trees and plants where you live, nature blazes in color and then settles to the color of stone: bare grey branches, grey waters, grey skies overhead. It's not winter yet, but it's near.

Autumn is as liminal, as change-oriented, as spring. But fall, as a harbinger of loss, has more negative undertones. With the autumn equinox in September, light and warmth start forsaking the Earth. Once we could count on our food waning, too. The harvest scythe traditionally carried by Death is a tool of autumn, not winter. (Imagine the Grim Reaper with a snow shovel instead, scooping up lives to toss them aside!) These losses summon melancholy, nostalgia, and apprehension.

Nonetheless, the season has glories. In fact, repeated surveys report that fall is Americans' favorite season.[1] It's possible the results reflect overwhelming seasonal PR driven by commercial interests—from back-to-school sales to pumpkin spice flavorings. Few seasons have been so exploited for a buck, and it's notable that autumn is considerably less popular in Britain, France, and Australia, for instance.[2] (Plus most of the U.S. surveys were conducted in fall, suggesting recency bias.) It's fair to call fall a time of contradictions, one that transitions from shocking colors to drab, from bounty to decay.

Cultures in Eastern geographies with late-summer monsoons often think of fall as a dry, breezy, and temperate time.

Autumn energies in brief: *Reaping and rejoicing over what's been brought to fruition, reflection (including nostalgia), releasing of what's no longer needed, and reinvestment for the future.*

They largely associate autumn with elements of earth, metal or, in the Ayervedic tradition, *vata* or air, which reflects the season's active or even anxious influences. In much of North America, however, fall presents as watery *kapha* instead: cooling, heavy, soft, and cloudy. Think of returning rains, growing dews, morning mists, or rot dissolving ripeness to mush. That's one reason this book follows traditions that assign water to autumn.

But fall's association with water is also about reflections and the uncertain depths of still pools. Water is a cross-cultural symbol of emotion, psyche, and the mysteries of the unconscious. As well-lit days of summer sink into shadows, our minds, too, may subside into more sober thoughts, misty memories, and fears of the unknown ahead.

In the seasons of human life, fall is sometimes aligned with maturity or adulthood. That leaves old age for hoary winter. But autumn often feels more akin to the teen years—when we're approaching maturity but typically still focused on self and emotions, with all the resulting drama and angst. Certainly the season features visual drama and angst, from flaming leaves passing on blustering winds to gloomy fog.

All these factors make autumn a season of strengthened community that also encourages introspection. We celebrate harvest bounty and communal learning, and we hold general elections to move toward shared goals. Yet we also start to withdraw from encroaching darkness into our homes, where we explore memory and hopes for the future. Accept Nature's invitation to bring work to culmination and celebrate before moving within to reflect and reset.

How to put autumn energy to work

▶ **Reinvest:** A key task of autumn in traditional times was setting aside part of the harvest for future seed. Creatives can benefit from that long-term perspective and use the back-to-school energy programmed into us as children. Take a class.

Fall is a time of contradictions... and a chance to slow down and look back.

Learn a new skill you might apply later. Start an idea file that can compost all winter. Or summon the Warrior archetype inside you and battle doubt or inertia to progress on projects you've let languish. Don't miss what amounts to a second chance to recommit to your creativity before the year ends, even if the results won't be immediate. See the activities called Ebb and Flow (p. 133), Indulge in Ideas (p. 145), and Go Deeper with Five Whys (p. 141).

▶ **Reap and rejoice:** Perhaps your hard work all year pays off now in a completed project. Take a cue from age-old harvest feasts and celebrate anything you've nurtured to ripeness. If necessary, expand your definition of what that might mean. Most creatives need to celebrate more, to recognize smaller milestones in a difficult endeavor that only occasionally ends in formal completions such as publication or a gallery show. Intermediate steps represent victories, too, whether that means finishing a chapter or gathering the nerve to seek feedback. Our brains respond to reward. In fact, research shows that the more people recognize they've made progress, the more productive they're likely to be, particularly in creative work.[3]

Autumn is associated with water, psyche, and emotion.

Need a nudge? Commit to working alongside and celebrating with creative friends. The concept of accountability buddies is widely used in creative communities to help get the work done. The same teamwork can help you identify milestones to celebrate and build creativity together while strengthening community spirit. Try the autumn activities called Flavor Your Work (p. 137), Befriend Your Monster (p. 147), or Trick Out Your Tombstone (p. 150) with friends.

▶ **Reflect:** Once the harvest is over, there's a chance to slow down and look back. Autumn has been called the time of reflection by everyone from artists to television producers.[4] What came to fruition in your creative life as a result of summer growth? What hasn't? Perhaps your skills have expanded. Other aspects of your creativity might remain constant—like your passion or purpose, for instance. Recognize and celebrate both the improvements and the consistencies that make your work unique. The activities called Examine Your Plate (p. 129), Unearth Secrets (p. 143), Catch Reflections (p. 139), Connect with Water (p. 135), and Decipher Wild Writing (p. 152) can help with this introspection.

▶ **Release:** If fall does anything, it reminds us that the abundance of summer cannot last indefinitely. Embrace change in your creative life, too. Like a tree dropping leaves, let go of something you're clutching. It may be a hopelessly overworked project or a bad habit you shouldn't wait for New Year's Eve to quit. Autumn is a more appropriate hour of reckoning, a partner to discernment in spring. (Consider Yom Kippur, usually in September or October, which formalizes the release of past mistakes before a fresh start.) Such release will free your fingers to grasp something new. Consider the activities in this section called Release What's No Longer Useful (p. 131) and Ebb and Flow (p. 133).

Note that giving is a form of releasing, a way to celebrate plenty by sharing it. This brings us back to autumn rejoicing in community. Share activities in this section with creative friends to make good use of the time that remains in the year.

Autumn is a season of strengthened community.

Autumn activities that follow:

Examine Your Plate 129
Release What's No Longer Useful 131
Ebb and Flow 133
Connect with Water 135
Flavor Your Work 137
Catch Reflections 139
Go Deeper with Five Whys 141
Unearth Secrets 143
Indulge in Ideas 145
Befriend Your Monster 147
Trick Out Your Tombstone 150
Decipher Wild Writing 152

Examine Your Plate

How this can help you: Clarify how you spend your time to better prioritize your creative work.

According to people who study such things, fear of failure is the number one barrier to creativity. But finding time for creative work, which also ranks highly,[5] is easily the top barrier mentioned by participants in the many workshops I've taken or led.

Or is time just an excuse to cover the fear? Trying to do and be too much is rampant in our culture, but there's a paradox at work here, too. Actress Lucille Ball apparently quipped, "If you want something done, ask a busy person to do it." Her counterintuitive quote is famous precisely because we know it's true. Artists who quit their "day jobs" often find they produced more when they didn't have the luxury of procrastination. Similarly, writers may crank out more words in the 30 minutes they can set aside daily during the week than in 4 hours stretching before them on a weekend. This sad truth is known colloquially as Parkinson's Law, which suggests tasks expand to fill the time available. It's certainly been true for me.

This activity can clarify how we're really using our time and lead to small changes for greater productivity. I recommend doing it with creative colleagues so you can compare your plates and share motivation and tips.

Why this activity fits fall: *This season of feasting increases awareness of how full our plates may be and the consequences of cramming in too much.*

Examine Your Plate—Step by Step

You'll need: A plain paper plate or other white circle, pens or pencils of various colors, a journal, and about 20 minutes.

1. **Get your hands on a white paper plate** or trace a circle on a blank sheet of paper.
2. **Around the edges of the circle, write, "My life plate."** This circle represents all your time and energy in a day, week, or month (or whatever period offers a representative average, considering your creative habits and other responsibilities).
3. **Imagine all your activities and responsibilities as foods** that will take space on your plate. List them alongside the plate. Include everything: the nourishing activities, such as creative or family time; yucky bits like chores that may be necessary; and junk food you indulge in but may regret (such as social media).

Wildly Inspired

4. Starting with your biggest time commitments, **draw a food shape or blob on your plate to represent each activity.** Draw bigger shapes for those that take the most attention. Add little things in the spaces left over. Use colors and words as helpful and fun.

5. When you're done, **consider the result, then answer these questions** in your journal. If you're doing this activity with companions, discuss your answers for extra insight.
    - What one word describes the overall impression given by your plate? *(For instance, balanced, overloaded, or chaotic.)*
    - How do you feel about this big picture and how well creativity fits in your life? *(For instance, does it give you more compassion for your busy self or nudge you to prioritize better?)*
    - Identify at least one thing on your plate you sometimes use to avoid creative work. Classes, research rabbit holes, and creative socializing are examples of worthwhile activities we may lean on too much. Are they hiding procrastination or secret insecurity?
    - What one item takes more space on the plate than you'd like?
    - What one item would you like to give more time and a bigger place on the plate?
    - What three steps could you take to bring these last two items into a better balance? (If it's something you'd like to remove altogether, the next activity could help.)

6. **Notice how you spend your time** over the next few days.
    - How accurate was your drawing? Often, the things we least want to prioritize (chores, social media, TV, driving) take even more of our time than we think.
    - How can you use this new awareness to support your creative work?

Release What's No Longer Useful

How this can help you: Use the power of ritual to consciously let go of something no longer serving you.

In nature, creativity cycles. From childhood, we learn that the leaves of deciduous trees fall because the tree no longer needs them. It's more scientifically accurate to say that as shorter days and cooler temperatures reduce the green chlorophyll in them, the leaves cost more energy to keep than they provide back to the tree. Even for evergreen trees, the oldest needles typically brown and drop in the fall.

These icons of autumn can remind us to deepen our acceptance of our own creative seasons. We've all got yellowing leaves draining energy better spent elsewhere. They may be unmet goals, self-defeating beliefs, low-value distractions, or projects you recognize as lost causes. Like trees, we need to cut loose such energy drains. Letting go can be hard, but this activity can help, especially when done with family or friends, who can help hold you accountable.

Why this activity fits fall: *It accepts nature's invitation to let go of what's not essential.*

Release What's No Longer Useful—Step by Step

You'll need: One or more real or paper leaves of good size, a writing implement (a Sharpie can do the job on real leaves), matches, and perhaps 20 minutes.

1. **Find one or more big, dry fallen leaves,** or make your own by tracing the big-leaf maple pattern on the next page onto paper.
2. **In the center of your leaf, write or draw something you need to release,** such as a frustrating creative project that realistically cannot be revived—at least for now.
3. **On one lobe or side of the leaf, note what that thing did for you while you had it.** (Most of the things we hold too long served us well once or in different circumstances.) Feel gratitude for what it taught you or any another purpose it served. *Examples: Improved prose skills or generated a character that could be used elsewhere.*
4. **On another lobe or side, write something of value you're choosing to replace it.** These might include time or energy to direct elsewhere (from a different project to better self-care), less frustration, etc.
5. **With ceremony, read what you wrote aloud.** (Remember, ritual signals to our subconscious minds that we're serious.)

Wildly Inspired

6. **Add the leaf to a backyard burn pile, set it alight in your fireplace or wood stove, or burn it over a candle** resting on an old cookie sheet so you can safely let go of the flaming leaf. Or, if you have a body of water nearby, move on to the next activity, Ebb and Flow, to release your leaf to the stream or waves while simultaneously asking for what might replace it. (Use a real leaf or dissolving rice paper for this option so your castoff doesn't wash up in someone else's life.)

7. **Focus on what you've chosen to move forward with** as noted in Step 4. Walk away without looking back.

Ebb and Flow

How this can help you: Extend the previous activity full circle and become more open to endings as a path to new starts and growth.

Every morning, I walk along a moody glacial river. Rain makes it smell like mud and surge the color of mocha. During freezes, the water clears and drops to reveal boulders. When it's high, it brings gifts from upstream: fallen logs, wood ducks, and commotion. It also steals things away: spawned-out salmon, misthrown dog balls, and the big-leaf maple "helicopters" that spin past my head during my autumn walks. Eventually my river reaches the sea, which has its own inbound gifts that may be carried off again later. Bodies of water are constant reminders of taking and giving in a reciprocal cycle.

Creative growth can be subject to similar cycles, trickling and then surging in response to the tides of our lives. The droughts, while frustrating, can be as valuable as the floods. In nature, many seeds—like those maple helicopters—must endure a period of cold and darkness before they will sprout. New ideas and habits may need a similar fallow time before they're ready to burst. In this light, autumn is a good time to give something up—to decay, to the flood of an outgoing tide—while planting a seed that can sprout in the future. Combining the two is a reciprocal act. What do you want? What will you give up to get it? One fertilizes and enables the other.

Why this activity fits fall: *It uses a watery metaphor and the season's ebbing energy to convert decay into reinvestment for the future.*

This activity uses these ideas to establish a balance. Give first to make room, and then ask to receive. This dual approach can help many creatives—who often struggle to feel deserving and may self-sabotage as a result—to welcome good fortune when it drifts their way.

Ebb and Flow—Step by Step

You'll need: Two found natural objects, an all-surface pen like a Sharpie, about 20 minutes, and a nearby body of water. If you don't live near any water, hold rains in mind and follow Option B in Step 4 instead.

1. **Find two natural items you can write on with a Sharpie,** such as dry leaves, smooth sticks, flat stones, or pieces of bark. The two items can be identical or different.
2. **On one, write a word or two or an image** that stands for something related to your creativity that you'd like the water to take away from your creative life.

Wildly Inspired

- + This might be an energy-draining thought or behavior, a project you need to release, or even a once-useful technique or genre that you need to move on from. Maybe someone else needs it, but you don't anymore.
- + Expect to apply some intention and effort. You're not asking for magic, just a little help from the flow.

3. **On the other item, write something you'd like flowing water to bring you,** from an idea to an award. Remember that even something floating into your life as a gift will require you to fish it out, so the gift you're requesting will involve work on your part, too.

4. **Option A: Take both items to your nearest body of water.** Using all your senses, observe the water a moment, noticing how it moves, what's left at its edges, and what it hides, reveals, and washes away. **Mindfully, throw the item representing the thing you're releasing as far into the water as you can.** (If it's too lightweight, such as a leaf may be, wrap it around a rock first or poke it under the surface with a stick.) Close your eyes and imagine the water accepting your gift.

   Option B: Take both items to a compost pile or loose soil in which you can dig. (Even a large houseplant's pot could work.) Using all your senses, observe that earth. Imagine rain falling, soaking in, and creating changes below the surface with time. **Dig a hole and bury the item** representing whatever you're releasing. Cover it mindfully and tamp down the soil. As you work, imagine the decay beginning already, breaking down whatever you're releasing and converting it to nutrients for new life.

5. Whether you followed Option A or Option B, **find a nearby patch of earth or sand.** Use a stick or your finger to draw a large, upside-down triangle there. In the center of this ancient symbol for water, **dig a small hole and bury the item representing what you'd like to receive.** Think of it as a seed. Cover it well to plant it, then splash a little water on the triangle to help your wish grow.

6. **Be patient.** Have faith in the Earth and its waters to wash away what's not needed, decide which seeds to sprout, and know when that time is right.

Connect with Water

How this can help you: Practice with observation, analogy, and metaphor while plumbing the depths of a primal relationship for insights that can be used in future art.

Years ago, on a long walking holiday in England, I amused myself by listening carefully to the creeks, rivers, raindrops, and surf that frequently accompanied or coursed over my path. Each water had its own voice, and I began to feel as though I could almost understand the stories and complaints shared by each. Creeks chattered away at their rocks, sharing gossip from farther upstream. Puddles I couldn't avoid squelched and squawked, some protesting the disturbance, while others, more welcoming, seemed reluctant to let me move on. Ocean waves snorted about what they'd seen on far shores and occasionally grumbled about going back. It was easy to understand why humans have for so long personified water. From the goddess Ganga to naiads, sea nymphs, and the like, we're attracted to water as a source of life while resenting its sometimes destructive power.

Why this activity fits fall: *It invokes reflection about deep emotions and dependencies through the reflective fall element of water.*

Does that remind you of anyone in your life?

When you hear "Mother Nature," you probably think first of the Earth and its plants, trees, and animals. But in many ways, Earth's waters offer a better maternal image. All life originally came from the seas—or so says our current best hypothesis. In the womb, we're suspended in amniotic water. The ocean echoes in the salty waters of our bodies, the tidal flow of our pulses and breath, and the emotions that wash over us or recede, toss us to new heights or drag us down.

As a result, we have a deep instinctual, even primal, relationship with water. This activity, adapted from suggestions in *Writing Wild* by Tina Welling, creates a parallel between potent water associations and the most primal of our nurturing human relationships. Use it to gain a new perspective on both. It might fuel unique expressions in your work.

Connect with Water—Step by Step

You'll need: A journal, a pen, something wet, and 20–30 minutes.

1. **Identify three different types of water, ways in which water moves, or something closely related**, from a downpour to a water strider. Ideally, go scout a puddle or creek or study a dripping faucet. Otherwise, note the first three wet images that spring to mind.

2. For each of your choices, **jot down key traits, sounds, sensations, or other impressions**. *For instance, a geyser explodes then goes quiet, may or may not be predictable, often smells bad, etc.*
3. **Pick one of the three that appeals most.** Considering any sounds, scents, or textures you may be able to sense or imagine, what does this thing seem to communicate to you? What ideas, emotions, or images does it represent for you? Note the answers in your journal.
4. **Now list the ways any of your choices relate to your mother** and your relationship with her, another mother figure in your life, or a nurturing figure in your current project.

    Wait, what? You read that right. Forced connections can be useful. Consider traits like flow, depths, resilience, surface tension, influence in your life, and the ability to soothe or revive.

    - If you had an initial emotional reaction to this suggestion, what was it? (Confusion, incredulity, snark?) Why?
    - What does that reaction say about your perception of the mother figure (or character) and how it's appropriate to think about them?
    - What does it say about your flexibility in making creative associations?

5. Continue to mine emotions and memories, and use your imagination as freely as needed to **find ways your mother (or the nurturing character) and your watery choices are different.**
6. **How would your mother (or the character) react** to your comparison and contrasts?
7. **If you were a variety of water** or watery element, what would it be? Why?
8. **Consider how you can use any insights from this exploration** to develop a female character or image in a current project.

Flavor Your Work

How this can help you: Surface emotional material for your work and better provoke your audience's senses and therefore emotional engagement.

From pumpkin spice and holiday cookies to the scents of woodsmoke, burning leaves, or fresh-cut evergreens, tastes and smells claim our attention during the harvest season. The two senses are closely entwined and strongly associated with memory.[6] This may be one of many reasons fall is considered a time of nostalgia. Autumn's weather conditions can increase our awareness of scents,[7] and emotions associated with those sensations rise from the past. Neuroscientists have confirmed the memory power of aromas and tastes, which is made possible by convenient brain anatomy plus the fact that both senses are active even before we're born.[8]

An industry known as scent branding capitalizes on this emotional and motivational power. Studies show that pleasant scents not only make consumers buy more and treat each other more kindly, they appear to improve how well our brains work.[9]

Draw on the same principles to summon the emotional power of tastes and smells in your work. If Marcel Proust could get a whole novel from a single bite of madeleine,[10] you can surface your own inspirations from other scents and tastes. Try it with the activity below.

Why this activity fits fall: *Taste and its dominant influence, smell, are the senses most associated with harvest and the season's typical nostalgia.*

Flavor Your Work—Step by Step

You'll need: A bite or two each of five different foods or items with fragrance, a pen, a journal, and 20–30 minutes.

1. **Assemble small amounts (about two bites each) of five different foods.** If you prefer, you can use items with fragrance that you smell during each step rather than taste.
    + Include a variety, such as sweet, salty, sour, savory, and crunchy. *(For instance, a nut, a slice of cheese, a bite of fruit, a flavored beverage, and a sauce or condiment.)* If you're working only with scent, consider sweet, spicy, floral, pungent, and biting, or any other combination of five.
    + Consider adding a few crackers, celery sticks, ice water, or the like as a palate-cleanser to use between flavors. For scents, a whiff of fresh air or your own skin works well.[11]

Wildly Inspired

2. Choose one of your samples. **Start by closing your eyes, smelling it, and noticing any associations or memories** that rise in your mind.
3. **Next, imagine that sample's history**—where and how it grew, the larger plant or animal it was once part of, and how it was made and transported to you.
4. **Taste it, chewing slowly before swallowing. Really experience it.** If you're using only your nose, try both deep inhalations and rapid sniff-sniffs, some with mouth closed and others with it open.
5. **Consider the sample's movement inside as its molecules slowly become part of you.** Feel how it connects you with its sources.
6. **Take a second bite and proceed to answer the questions below** in your journal, relating your answers to a current project or character if you like. There's a different question for each taste.

   Repeat Steps 2 through 6 as you move on to each sample. Enjoy a palate-cleanser between if you like.

   - First sample: What words or images does your experience of this sample prompt?
   - Second sample: Associate this sample's taste (or smell) with an emotion. Which one and why?
   - Third sample: Associate this sample's taste or smell with an action. Use your imagination if needed. Which action and why?
   - Fourth sample: Pretend you have synesthesia, in which senses merge and colors may be experienced as textures or sounds, for instance. Associate the flavor or scent of this sample with a sound, shape, or both. What is it, and why?
   - Fifth sample: What memory do you associate with this sample?

7. *Storytellers:* **Write a memory prompted by a flavor or scent into a scene**. Use either your own point of view or that of a character you're working with. Incorporate a few of the emotions, actions, or other responses that rose during this activity.
8. See if you can **bring the enhanced awareness of this activity into your daily eating as well as your work.**

Catch Reflections

How this can help you: Become more aware of half-conscious priorities and concerns so they can guide your creative work.

One fall afternoon, I took a journal to a nearby riverbank to explore the associations that can rise between our states of mind and our external surroundings. I began playing with the activity you'll find below, inspired in part by another exercise in *Writing Wild* by Tina Welling. It's easy to simply note what triggers your senses, and because it grounds you in your body, it's a useful technique for lowering stress.[12] Like the Summer activity called Ask for a Sign, this one draws on our brain's habit of filtering out information it doesn't deem relevant to the moment.[13] Instead of passively accepting what gets past the gate, it's useful to consider *why* what you notice might be relevant now and how our perceptions of the world at any moment reflect our own inner landscapes.

Why this activity fits fall: *Autumn's slow decline encourages reflection and turning within to pay more attention to what's under the surface.*

I soon had a long list of riverside sights, sensations, and the antics of my dog, who amused herself with a stray ball nearby until I did something more interesting for her. As I examined the items on my list and thought about why I'd noticed those first among the thousands of possibilities, connections jumped out at me, including a few that seemed counterintuitive. My dog's ball clicked with the smooth stones in the river, for instance, while the words "playful" and "self-amused" seemed to describe both the dog and me, too. Similarly, the splash of a spawning salmon echoed to me of creative ideas bubbling up from the depths.

There are less positive impressions in my list too, such as feeling chilly, the hard rock I sat on, and the distant noise of traffic. But those felt less important, not worth spending time on. One that caught my eye more: "alone." I'd jotted that word near the top of my list but it wasn't accurate. My dog was with me. When I noticed the contradiction, I realized that feeling of isolation was actually my fear that the activities in this book won't speak to anyone else.

Just then, another fish splashed. I decided to treat it as a confirmation to keep trusting the forces that rise from the depths. Try this activity particularly when you're tired, discouraged, or unsure what to do next. The answers swimming just below your awareness might apply in surprising ways.

Catch Reflections—Step by Step

You'll need: A journal, a pen, and 20–30 minutes.

1. **Sit somewhere quietly with your journal,** either outdoors or near a window. Close your eyes, breathe deeply, feel centered and calm. Let your mind wander gently over your current project without focusing on any particular aspect of it.
2. Open your eyes. **As quickly as you can, jot down the first 15–30 things that capture your attention,** internal or external, using all your senses. When you need to pause more than a few seconds to identify the next thing, stop.
3. Look back over the list. **Circle a handful that jump out at you,** seem most important, or strike you as unusual—perhaps things you wouldn't ordinarily notice.
4. **Draw lines between or otherwise connect any that are related** through meaning, associations, or emotions.
5. **Consider the following questions**, journaling the answers if you like.
   - Across most of the list, is there an overall mood or theme? How does that mood reflect your own right now?
   - Which things on your list, if any, are symbols with particular meaning for you or that you've used in creative work?
   - Are there any pairs that seem contradictory in mood or meaning? How might that reflect any confusion or ambivalence you're feeling?
   - What memories does any circled item prompt? How might that memory relate to your life or work now?
   - Does any item appear somehow in your current project? Should one?
   - How might something on this list answer a question or solve a current problem in your work or your life?

Go Deeper with Five Whys

How this can help you: Clarify deeper emotional drivers to explore your motivations or strengthen characters and story tension.

My years in Corporate America contained a few lessons with surprising application to real life. For instance, I buy little in bulk because I know about the hidden costs of inventory, and the Douglas squirrels that take winter shelter in my garage don't let me forget. Spare toilet paper shredded for nesting material is proof that buying more than will fit in the bathroom wastes money. Businesses call it "inventory shrink."

An even better corporate lesson for creatives is, "Ask why five times." This problem-solving technique reveals root causes to fix fundamental issues rather than pasting band-aids on symptoms. Say you're taking a test and keep breaking the tip of your pencil. Why? Because you're pushing down too hard on the paper. Why? Because you're tense. Why? Because you're afraid you'll fail the test. Why? Because you didn't study. Why? Because squirrels shredded your textbook for nesting material. We could keep asking why—five may need to be 10—but if you didn't ask why at least five times, you might think you had a faulty pencil or needed anxiety meds when the real problem requires a rather different solution.

Why this activity fits fall: *The season encourages reflection and plunging beneath emotional surfaces.*

This technique isn't merely practical. It's useful for exploring emotions and motivations—our own or those of characters. The technique is also helpful when you feel blocked or have lost sight of what first sparked a project (see Sweep Clean in Spring). Using it can help us create stronger, more motivated characters or bring more of ourselves to our work to deepen it emotionally and make it more universal.

Go Deeper with Five Whys—Step by Step

You'll need: A journal, a pen, and 20–30 minutes.

1. **Identify which character you want to work with** (including yourself). Protagonists are the obvious choice, but most important characters are worth understanding better. That includes yourself as a creative.
2. **Answer *all* of the following questions** for the character or yourself as an artist. If you struggle to answer or understand a question, jot down whatever rises, ask why you're struggling with that one in particular, or ask yourself another question that seems to fit better.

- First, what does this character want or think they want?
- Why is that goal important or meaningful to them?
- Okay, but why do they *really* want it? What does it represent emotionally, psychologically, or socially that they need?
- Why do they need that deeper gain or achievement? In other words, why don't they have that inherently, or why is the deeper psychological reward or emotion not immediately available to them?
- Why is that deeper reward or emotion significant for *you*? Why are you making it part of the project?
- Why is the person or situation that's blocking the character preventing an easy resolution? (What's working against your character, and why?)
- Why isn't the character succeeding (so far) in going through or around the blocker? (This might be a character flaw, an opponent, or a lack of correct information, for instance.)
- Why, then, is the character still hoping or trying?
- Finally, a few whats:
    - What, then, are they attempting instead? Why won't that initially work?
    - What will the character ultimately be willing to do to get what they want?
    - What price will they pay (or what will they lose) in the process?

3. **Use the information you learn** to move ahead with your creative work!

Unearth Secrets

How this can help you: Identify secrets from your life that might shape motivations and intrigue in your work—or secrets about your creative practice that hold you back.

If there's a season for revealing secrets, it's autumn. It starts with potatoes brought to light by a harvesting shovel, but it doesn't end there. Ghosts manifest to reveal old injustices. Long-forgotten corpses claw their way into the light. In more mundane realms, new clothing trends are displayed in fall Fashion Week. TV networks premiere new shows, and mystery novels launch for readers evading fall's gloomy weather.[14] Finally, before fall is over, Advent calendars reveal a secret each day to count down toward winter's first day.

Secrets are a creative's best friend. One lesson that's plain in British TV mysteries: The plot thickens when every character has something to hide, related to the murder or not. Secrets obscure motivations, complicate interactions, and make the innocent behave in ways that look guilty. This truth can enrich art of other kinds, too—think of the delight of finding Easter eggs in a video game or discovering unexpected details in classic paintings.[15] This activity can help you leverage the power of secrets to add depth and surprise to your work.

Why this activity fits fall: *It focuses on the psychological aspects of our lives and explores what may hide beneath.*

Unearth Secrets—Step by Step

You'll need: A journal, a pen, and plenty of time to muse.

1. Perhaps on a pleasant autumn walk, **consider a secret you discovered,** recently or in childhood. (Complete this activity for yourself, for a character, or both by using your own life as material for a character's story.) Answer these questions in your journal:
    - What was the secret?
    - If someone asked you to keep it, did you? Why or why not?
    - Were you glad to find out, or did you wish the secret had stayed buried? Why?
    - How did the knowledge affect your behavior, a relationship, or your attitude toward secrets today?
    - What image or symbol might you associate with this secret?
2. **How could you use a version of that secret**—or one of your own that you kept from others—to enrich characters, scenes, or situations in your work? What details might you change to make it work for your project while retaining its emotional impact?

Wildly Inspired

3. **What's one secret about your creative life or current project** that you wouldn't want anyone to know—or perhaps have been hiding from yourself? (For instance, do you suspect you don't have enough talent or aren't willing to do all the hard work required?)
   - Is it a truth or simply a fear? What evidence do you have either way?
   - What would happen if anyone else found out?
   - If a creative friend admitted this secret to you, what would you do or say? How does that compare with what you imagined above? (We're usually far harder on ourselves than others would be.)
   - If someone did find out, what would you say or do next?

4. **Consider writing your secret (in code or with symbols if need be) on a fallen leaf and releasing it** with the activity called Release What's No Longer Useful (p. 131).

5. *Extra credit for storytellers*:

   ☐ **Write a scene** in which one character confides this secret to a pet, tree, or other confidant. What or who do they tell, and why? How do their feelings change as a result?

   ☐ **Write a scene** in which a character with a secret tries to determine if another person already knows it or not. Or, better yet, find a friend and together act out this scene.
   - + Pay attention to how the secret affects tone of voice, subtext, and tension between them. (This can help you develop characters even if the secret has no part in your story.)
   - + As the scene progresses, let the secret slip—either the secret-keeper makes a mistake or the other person already knows. How do the dynamics between them change?

   ☐ Using what you've learned in this activity, **give your protagonist and your primary antagonist each a potent secret,** even if it will never be revealed in your story. Then write (or rewrite) one or more scenes in which their respective secrets are on their minds and they fear revelation. How might that affect the rest of the story?

Indulge in Ideas

How this can help you: Experience the value of pushing past easy answers to more unusual and creative solutions.

As fall weather turns cool, mice and small Douglas squirrels take shelter among the rafters of my garage. All winter long and into the spring, I find sunflower seeds, dried kernels of corn, and stolen dog kibble cached in places like workbench drawers and unworn boots. My wild tenants store more than they could ever eat. They get caught up in the excess of autumn.

From Halloween candy and pumpkin spice deodorant to the entire Thanksgiving scene, fall is the season of overindulgence. Going too far has a place in creativity, too—one we're less likely to regret. As scientist Linus Pauling said, "The best way to have a good idea is to have a lot of ideas."[16] This activity pushes you to "keep going" past your initial sense of completion to more surprising and perhaps more creative results. It can be fun and enlightening to do with a small group, whether everyone uses the same object or not, if you share and discuss your results.

Why this activity fits fall: *It aligns with the season's spirit of plenty and encourages harvesting only the best.*

Indulge in Ideas—Step by Step

You'll need: A journal, a pen, and about 30 minutes. A timer may also be useful.

1. **Pick up a small object, such as something you might find outdoors** (whether naturally or mysteriously). It might be a leaf or rock, for instance, or a button or key. This activity is particularly fruitful if you select something that does or could have a role in a current or new project, even if only as part of a setting.

2. Sit or stand somewhere you can write. **As quickly as you can, list 10 ways of describing, using, or thinking about the item.** (If you're a visual artist, you might list 10 ways to depict it, whether that means perspectives on it or media choices, or make 10 quick sketches from different perspectives and scales). If you have trouble going fast, use a timer to build pressure and give yourself no more than 1 or 2 minutes.

    + *For example, a maple "helicopter" might be eaten, stuck between lips like a toothpick, used as a bookmark, etc. Or you might describe it as furry, sticky, blade-shaped....*

    + List the "bad" or inaccurate notions that rise, too. Many people prematurely judge or reject ideas, blocking the imagination. If this describes you, don't fight it. Instead, simply list 10 ideas *plus* 10 "bad" ideas for each step. Whether they're really no good can be determined later, when a "bad" one might surprise you—or prompt something better.

Wildly Inspired

3. **Move to another location, taking your item with you.** Spend 30 seconds using your senses to notice how this location is different in sensations, mood, or purpose.
4. Resetting a timer as needed, **list 10 more ways** to describe or use your same subject. Push yourself. It's okay if your list includes things that seem random or even nonsensical.
5. **Move to a third location.** After experiencing this latest place for 30 seconds, turn your attention to your subject and list 10 more.
    + If this feels hard, give yourself more constraints, not fewer. Considerable research[17] shows that, rather than making creativity harder, constraints promote more unusual solutions. So consider limiting yourself to answers that directly relate to your surroundings, for instance, or use only words that start with vowels.
6. Review your whole list and **circle the most interesting or unexpected** ways you found. Why do they appeal? How many are in the first 10 versus the last 10?
7. Examine any words, descriptions, or perspectives that don't make obvious sense. **Explore deeper associations or memories** that suggest why they rose for you and how they might actually be unique and perfect.
8. Create a short paragraph, poem, or drawing that **captures the item using one of the unusual connections** you like best.
9. **Consider other ways to immerse yourself in ideas** to increase the chances of your own stroke of genius.

For instance, an illustrator friend of mine draws and posts a monster a day in October, and other artists have taken up his challenge. A similar "one a day" brainstorming concept informs a writing community event currently called StoryStorm that was created by author Tara Lazar. Her event, which once took place in November, now happens in January, which is not what I'd call the ideal seasonal timing. But it's still a great model for gathering and stashing ideas as the seeds of future work. Follow suit by spending a few minutes each day for a month capturing a new character, image, setting, or a single evocative line of writing.

Or try the approach of creatives who keep a journal, clipping file, or box of ideas. Even if you never return to them, you can be sure they're composting in your subconscious to fertilize future work.

Befriend Your Monster

How this can help you: Access semiconscious beliefs and fears so you can deal with them and help useful answers arise from deeper inside.

Most creative people have monsters inside that make it harder to be creative. These monsters include fears of failure, emotional vulnerability, and even success. The scariest may be our own deep, dark hungers—for approval, validation, belonging, or love—or other parts of ourselves we mostly stuff away in the shadows.

We may not see these terrors, but we hear their voices too often. Do you recognize any of these common artistic monsters? In truth, they often want to protect us but go about it all wrong.

Why this activity fits fall: *It taps the liminal creative power of Halloween.*

- **The Perfectionist Phantom.** Perfectionism, sometimes attributed to the inner critic, often masks a fear of failure. If you never release your work to an audience, you can never hear that your best effort is not (yet) good enough—or maybe never will be. But too much protection backfires.
- **The Self-Sabotage Slime.** For some artists, fear of success is real, too. Achieving dreams may move us into unknown territory. Fellow artists or family members may display jealousy. Subconsciously, it can seem safer to stick with the status quo. This monster ensures we don't make time for the work, research the market, stay ahead of deadlines, or carefully follow submission rules, for instance.
- **Franken-Failure**, aka the Warty Waste of Time. Not all fear of failure makes us too careful. Instead, this monster distracts, claims we're wasting time or being selfish, or threatens other identities (frequently "the good mom") to block us from committing time to our crafts.
- **The Heartbreak Horror.** Years ago, a friend who'd written several unsold comedies started a darker manuscript that wowed all who read it. We cheered her on, certain it would lead to a book deal, but she quit working on it, citing the painful memories she'd drawn on. Unfortunately, that's often where the best art lies, and I don't think it's a coincidence she hasn't yet been published. Fear of digging up feelings we'd rather leave buried prevents some artists from creating their best work.
- **The One-Eyed, One-Hit Wonder.** Many artists would be thrilled to have even one hit! Yet society mocks those without enduring success, even if markets, trends, or timing deserve more blame than talent. As a result, few newly recognized artists avoid the terror of being unable to follow one success with another.
- **The Icky Imposter.** This one plagues many no matter how much they've achieved. They work in fear that the next project might finally prove them an imposter. A glimpse of this beast can be motivating, but more may be paralyzing.

A Warty Frankenmonster paralyzed me for a while as I worked—or, more accurately, did not work—on this book. It took several attempts, but eventually I recognized my monster. I call him Weird Wally. He tells me my work is too offbeat to interest anyone else. He's grown fat on years of rejection after early success.

Even after I spotted and began dodging him, I realized that to fend him off, I'd begun writing from my head instead of my heart. That way rejection, if it still came, wouldn't feel so personal.

The results were predictably boring, and my muse departed for a warmer climate. When I figured out why—I'd veered away from this book's inspiration—I knew I had to make friends with Weird Wally, the wart-covered fear that anything I wrote would fall flat. Only then could I access the passion and personal voice this project, to have any chance, demanded. Whatever the result, at least I'd be true to my original vision. Better to be rejected for who you are than for trying and failing to be someone else!

As soon as I realized this and gave poor, lonely Wally a hug of acceptance, my muse began whispering again. Perhaps we're only creating activities for a few friends to enjoy, but that's enough.

It's useful to confront monsters like Wally (and everyone has at least one). Acknowledging them drains their power. Having fun with this activity is the first step. I encourage you to do this activity for yourself as a creative, but if you're not ready, you can work through it for a character instead.

Either way, try it in the evening, perhaps by the light of a candle. Daylight and rational thinking send our deepest fears skittering for the shadows. But that's where they do the most harm. Lure them out gently to defuse them.

Befriend Your Monster—Step by Step

You'll need: A sheet of blank paper, colored pens or pencils, the 8-minute meditation recorded for you at https://youtu.be/OP8kN2zIq20, a journal, about 45 minutes, and an optional lit candle.

1. On one side of your paper, **write out this question**: "What inner monster is threatening me lately, and how does it hinder me as I try to achieve my goals?"
2. **Skip a few lines of space and write**, "What more do I know about this monster and where it comes from?"
3. Pick up a pen of a different color and **go back to the first question. Try to answer it** in a few sentences. Be honest. No one else needs to see it.
4. Now, **switch your pen to your nondominant hand.** Use that hand to write or draw answers to the second question. Don't worry about legibility; you'll know what you're trying to write.
5. Put your pen down for a moment and close your eyes. **Notice any tension, unease, tingling, or other sensations in your body** prompted by these questions. Explore them without trying

to stop them. Put a hand over them and reassure yourself that you're safe. Then open your eyes and proceed.

6. Pick up a pen of a third color. **Still using your nondominant hand, answer this new question:** "How does this monster think it's protecting me, even when it doesn't feel like help?" If necessary, speculate by starting out, "Maybe it wants to..."

7. Pick up a different color or two. Still **using your nondominant hand, draw something that represents your monster**—a shape or symbol, its face, or a scribble capturing the sensations it has caused in your body.

8. Turn over your page and put down your pens.

9. **Listen to the recorded "Meet Your Monster" meditation** at https://youtu.be/OP8kN2zIq20 and take notes as instructed.

10. When you've finished the meditation, take a deep breath and perhaps stand and **shake off any lingering hair, scales, or smell your monster left behind.** If you worked by candlelight, turn up the electric lights. You're safe here, out of reach of your monster, and better equipped to move forward.

11. Review your notes and drawings, including what you did with your nondominant hand. Make any needed notes or clarifications, then **answer these questions** in a journal:

    - What surprised you in your writing, your drawing, or your conversation with the monster?
    - What did you learn about yourself (or your character) and any barriers to overcome?
    - How does your body feel now? Any change in the sensations you noticed in step 5?

12. **Consider spending more creative time with your monster.** Art supplies of any sort could help bring your monster further into the light while you build a more equitable relationship with it.

    On the other hand, if your conversation with your monster was not helpful, consider using the activity called Release What's No Longer Useful (p. 131) to send it away.

Trick Out Your Tombstone

How this can help you: Playful visualization of your own legacy tones imaginative skills while increasing perspective and focus to generate energy for a productivity surge.

Few in Western civilization consider autumn without also thinking of Halloween, Dia de los Muertos, All Saint's Day, or the Celtic festival of Samhain. These events coincide with the sun's cross-quarter day, halfway between fall equinox and winter solstice. For the Celts, this astronomical event marked the start of winter. Others consider it a seasonal midpoint—in this case, mid-autumn.

Why this activity fits fall: *Like Halloween, it contrasts harvest plenty with the unknowns ahead, confronting fears while celebrating life.*

Cross-cultural traditions for this transitional (liminal) time include beliefs about the relative nearness of the Otherworld or underworld and the value of masks, invisibility, role-reversals, and trickery to evade the resulting danger. (See the introduction to Spring on p. 55 for more about liminality.) As winter looms, the most pressing danger is death, evident in denuded trees, waning daylight, and rotting plants all around us. Confronting this fear is a highlight of the season, with ritualized visits to death—from dressing as zombies to fool the Reaper to mollifying small monsters with candy. These strengthen our resolve to survive and the community connections that help while renewing our awareness of our own present vibrancy.

Author and mythologist Michael Meade connected such rituals to a kind of rebirth when he wrote that, traditionally, "the village of the underworld was secretly connected to the source of life. The willingness to go there meant entering the oldest ritual of the world, where releasing the corpse of one's life leads to the renewal of the golden self within."[18] Use the same principle in this activity to renew the golden spirit of your creativity to come.

Trick Out Your Tombstone—Step by Step

You'll need: A pen, a journal, and 30–45 minutes.

1. If you can, **visit a nearby cemetery**, or at least get somewhere outside. Notice sounds, smells, and other sensations of fall, such as woodsmoke, moldering leaves, a new chill in the breeze, the passing school bus that was absent all summer.
2. Now **imagine a most unusual cemetery** designed especially for creatives. It might combine aspects of a garden and an art gallery, library, amusement park—or all three. Perhaps there are a few traditional headstones, but among them are tombs in all shapes

and sizes, from pianos to giant books, hologram dancers to wandering minstrels—symbols of many creative passions. (This is not as strange as you may think. Real monuments today include BMW replicas, a giant mosaic cat, a great white shark, and other surprising sculptures.[19]) Visitors walk among and climb on these intriguing legacies.

3. Pretend neither money nor public opinion could affect your decision. You've got the luxury package, prepaid. In your journal, **answer the following questions about what you'd like added to this memory park as a lasting symbol of your existence.** (If you've previously completed the Winter activity called Gnaw Your Creative Bone on p. 168, you might also refer to those answers for ideas.)

   - What, if anything, would be engraved on your monument for others to read? In addition to any epitaph, might you offer observers a curse, a poem, advice, a list of your awards, or a line from your best review?
   - How does your tombstone display, represent, or exemplify your creative work? Your luxury monument includes the multi-media option, so what sounds, scents, or tactile experiences might remind your adoring fans of your life and work?

   For instance, my ideal headstone might include copies of my books for visitors to read, but its most important feature will be a line borrowed from the movie Spinal Tap: *"She went to 11." Why? Because I lost a sibling when we were both very young, so I've long felt I needed to try many things and experience enough life for us both. I'm proud of my books, but going to 11, in writing and other adventures, has been even more central to my life and identity. For that reason, my marker would also include a rope swing, tree fort, steep slide, or some other means of active adventure.*

   - What supportive family members, muses, or artistic inspirations might your monument name?
   - Where in the cemetery would it be located? (Beneath a tree, alongside someone famous, floating overhead?)
   - It can be fruitful—or amusing!—to ask other creatives who know you and your work well what they might expect to see on your tombstone or what they'd suggest if the decision were theirs. Even if you don't bother asking, what do you think they might say?

4. If you like, **draw your monument or tombstone** in your journal.
5. Look back at your answers. **How can you express more of your monument's energy and spirit in your work?**
6. **What more do you really want to get done** before it's time for this imaginary monument to be placed?
7. **Go do it.** Or at least schedule a specific time this week to make progress.

Decipher Wild Writing

 *How this can help you:* Stretch your imagination and perhaps intuit a message you need to hear.

As a kid—like all kids?—I loved secret codes. I imagined the stars as notes in a musical score we could play, if only we knew where to draw the lines of the staff. Years later, when I read Susanna Clarke's *Jonathan Strange & Mr Norrell*, I could barely get past her splendid idea that a scattering of birds in the sky might similarly represent writing with meaning. That was the book's climax for me. I wanted to be magician enough to decipher such a message from the wild.

Why this activity fits fall: *This is a season where things that have been hidden may be revealed.*

It's not such a crazy idea. Our natural environment sends countless encoded messages some creatures receive but we miss. The declarations pounded out by the flicker on my chimney flashing each spring use a Morse code only his potential girlfriends can translate. Even more mysterious are the colors and scents we can't discern at all, the shifts in pressure and magnetism and radiation we can detect only with machines. What might be revealed to us if we had a dog's nose, a bat's ears, a whale's sense of direction?

Though we're stuck making do with the senses we have, autumn is still a rich time for secrets revealed. Every season has its own revelations, of course, from the new sprouts of spring to the activity of wild rabbits that remain unobserved until tracks in winter snow give them away. But fall delivers particularly striking revelations. The fruiting bodies of fungi suddenly erupt into sight. The nests of squirrels and birds, once shrouded by leaves, emerge with the skeletal branches of trees. Dew spotlights the webs of spiders who've worked unsuspected all summer. Frost begins tagging windshields with pale graffiti. This activity plays with messages in nature you may not have noticed when the world looked more lush. While it can't give you senses you don't already have, it draws on one you can use without limit: your imagination. Try it to explore what you most need to hear from the world—perhaps a message of encouragement from deep within your own heart.

Decipher Wild Writing—Step by Step

You'll need: A journal, 20 quiet minutes, a pen, and one of the images here or one of your own that you find.

Fall Inward

1. **Choose a mysterious image** that calls to you, using one of the suggestions on these pages or something you find or have photographed—a unique cloud formation, ocean spray, etc.
2. **Sit with your encoded message somewhere quiet,** preferably outdoors.

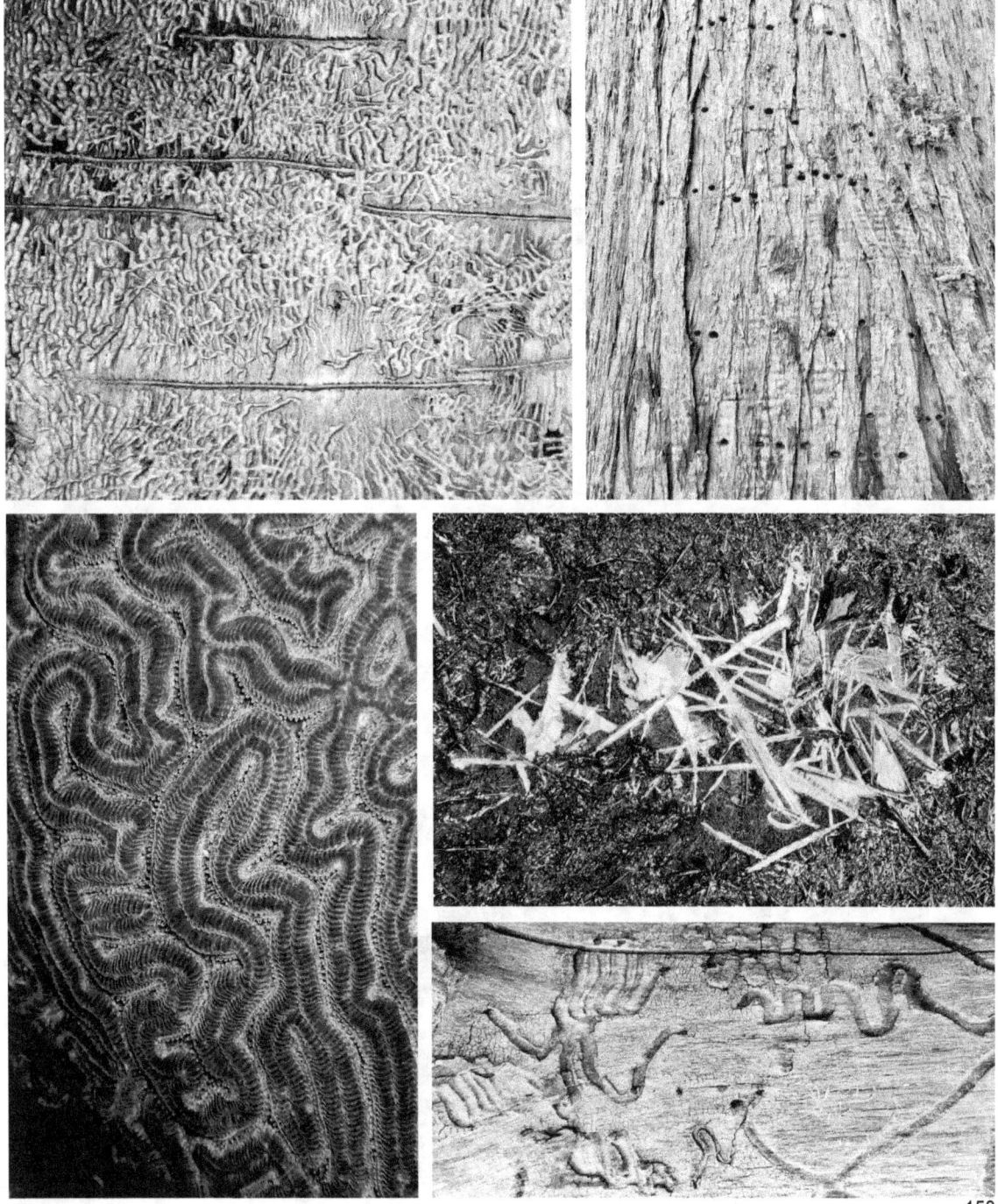

Wildly Inspired

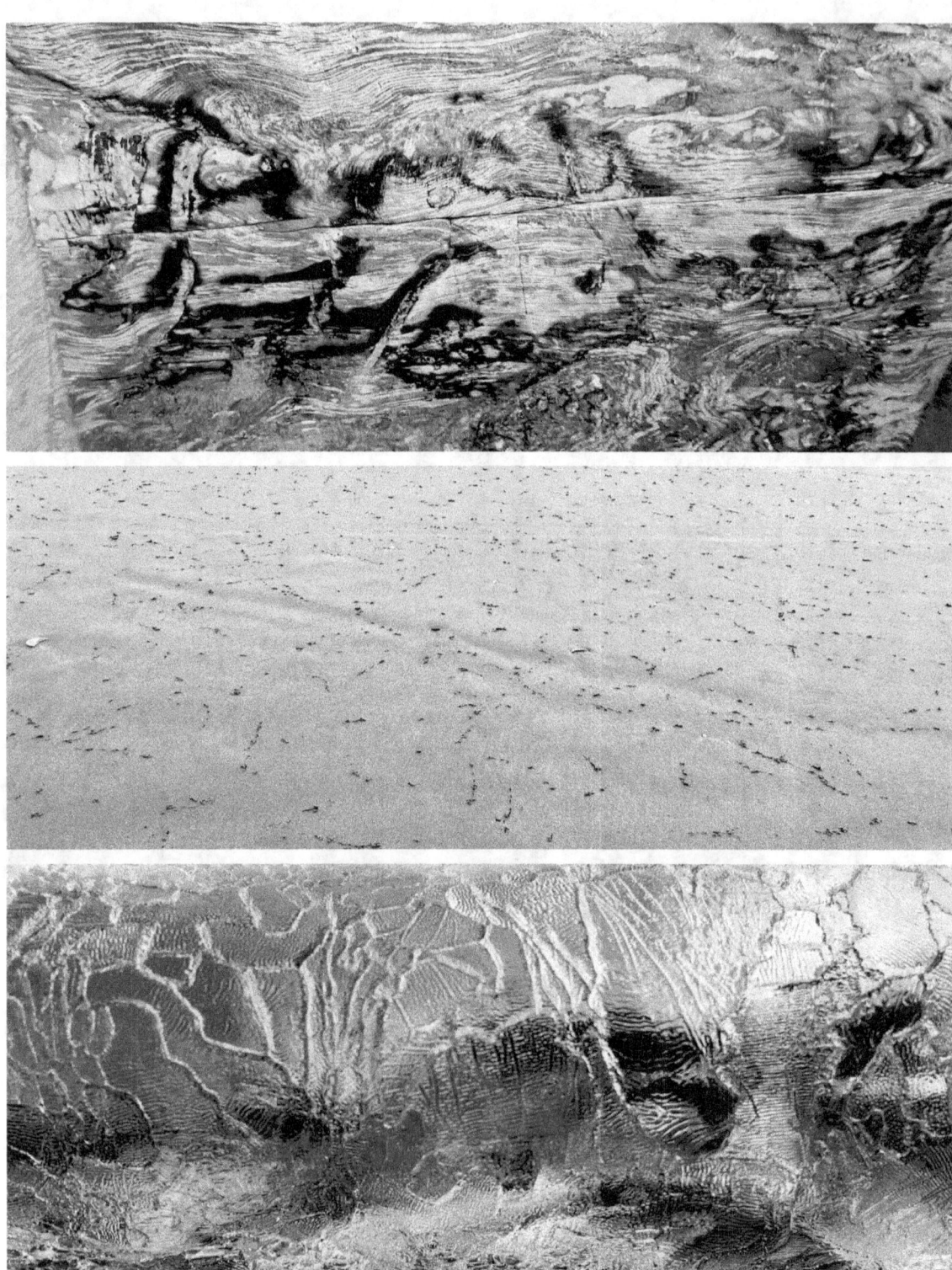

Fall Inward

3. **Start by noticing the sensory evidence of life around you.** This might include a whiff of scent or the sound of a machine. Consider how each is a message to someone. *(A car engine may tell a dog a beloved person has arrived home, for instance.)*
4. **Observe your encoded message obliquely**. Try glancing in short bursts, using peripheral vision, turning the image upside down, or thinking in symbols such as hobo signs. Imagine what the message's creator might have to say—or what your own intent would have been if you had created it.
5. Use your intuition and imagination to **decipher the writing as though it's a message specifically for you**. In your journal, write what it says. Be as playful or as heartfelt as you like.
6. **What might you say or do in response?**
7. **Follow any resulting directive or impulse for creative work.** *(For example, see my poem below, written about worm-scored wood, and thanks for indulging me.)*

Decipher This Writing

Decipher this scrawl.
Like the murmuring sea,
It carries a message for you.

Or if you prefer—
If a city's your thing—
Translate the skyline at dusk.
The world hides a memo there, too.

For headlights on highways
And beetles in trees
Signify more than mere chance.

They're songs in the voice
Of the soul of the Earth—
Love notes from Nature,
Invitations to dance.

Consider the answer
You'll give in reply.
Respect truly never goes wrong,

So charm her with wonder
And return her wild love
To add your own voice to the song.

Autumn Endnotes

1—See endnote 1 in the Spring section, plus Palmer, Kate. "Fall Is Favorite Season for Most Americans." *YouGov*, June 13, 2010

2—"The Days May Be Getting Shorter, but Summer Is Still Britain's Favourite Season." *Ipsos*. 20 September 2024. https://www.ipsos.com/en-uk/days-may-be-getting-shorter-summer-still-britains-favourite-season; "Ranking of Favorite Seasons in France in 2018," *Statista*, July 4, 2024. https://www.statista.com/statistics/947024/favorite-season-in-france; Sharwood, Anthony. "Revealed: Australia's Favourite Season." *Weatherzone*, June 22, 2022. https://www.weatherzone.com.au/news/revealed-australias-favourite-season/648578

3—Amabile, Teresa M., and Kramer, Steven J. "The Power of Small Wins." *Harvard Business Review*. May 2011. https://hbr.org/2011/05/the-power-of-small-wins; McNally, Melanie A. "From Small Steps to Big Wins: The Importance of Celebrating." *Psychology Today*, June 12, 2024. https://www.psychologytoday.com/us/blog/empower-your-mind/202406/from-small-steps-to-big-wins-the-importance-of-celebrating

4—For instance, artist Thomas D. Mangelson, composer Jennifer Higdon, educator Anna LeMind, and television producer Mitchell Burgess

5—Much of the writing on the supposed top barriers to creativity is unscientific or based on research too granular to be generally useful, but supporting resources include Morais, M. D. F., et al. "Inventory of Barriers to Personal Creativity: A Validation Study Involving University Students." *Cognitive, Social, and Behavioural Sciences*, icCSBs 2014 (Eds: Z. Bekirogullari, & M. Y. Minas), vol 1. *European Proceedings of Social and Behavioural Sciences*, pp. 135-145. https://doi.org/10.15405/epsbs.2014.05.16; Chacón-López, Helena, and Maeso-Broncano, Ana. "Creative Development, Self-Esteem and Barriers to Creativity in University Students of Education According to Their Participation in Artistic Activities." *Thinking Skills and Creativity*, Vol. 48 (2023), pp. 101270. https://doi.org/10.1016/j.tsc.2023.101270

6—Spence, C. "Just How Much of What We Taste Derives from the Sense of Smell?" *Flavour* 4:30 (2015). https://doi.org/10.1186/s13411-015-0040-2; Walsh, Colleen. "What the Nose Knows," *The Harvard Gazette*. February 27, 2020

7—Walder, Nadine. "Effects of Weather and Humidity on Your Sense of Smell." Stadler Form blog, July 31, 2023. https://www.stadlerform.com/en/health/aromatherapy/effects-of-weather-and-humidity-on-your-sense-of-smell

8—Ustun, B., et al. "Flavor Sensing in Utero and Emerging Discriminative Behaviors in the Human Fetus." *Psychological Science*, 33:10 (2022), pp. 1651-1663. https://doi.org/10.1177/09567976221105460; Palmer, Jacqueline S. "Sensing in the Womb." *The American Biology Teacher*, 49: 7 (1987), pp. 411–25. https://doi.org/10.2307/4448576

9—Archer, James. "Let Them Sniff, Customers Will Buy More." *Inc.* Jan. 23, 2013. https://www.inc.com/james-archer/let-them-sniff-customers-will-buy-more.html; Minsky, Laurence, et al. "Inside the Invisible but Influential World of Scent Branding." *Harvard Business Review*, April 11, 2018. https://hbr.org/2018/04/inside-the-invisible-but-influential-world-of-scent-branding

10—In Proust's *Remembrance of Things Past* or *À La Recherche du Temps Perdu*, which is the origin of what's now known as a Proustian moment.

11—There's conventional wisdom about scent palate cleansers, especially coffee, but data about what actually works is weak. Grosofsky, A., et al. "An Exploratory Investigation of Coffee and Lemon Scents and Odor Identification." *Perceptual and Motor Skills*, 112:2 (2011), pp. 536-538. https://doi.org/10.2466/24

12—Shukla, Aditya. "A Five-Step Mindfulness Grounding Technique to Ease Anxiety and Why Mindfulness Works." *Cognition Today*, Nov. 26, 2019, updated March 27, 2020. https://cognitiontoday.com/5-step-mindfulness-grounding-technique-to-ease-anxiety-why-it-works; Finck, Carolyn, et al. "A Multisensory Mindfulness Experience: Exploring the Promotion of Sensory Awareness as a Mindfulness Practice." *Frontiers in Psychology* vol. 14:1230832, Nov. 9, 2023. https://doi.org/10.3389/fpsyg.2023.1230832

13—See endnote 12 in the Summer section for more about mental filtering.

14—A large percentage of new fiction is launched in the fall for holiday shopping. Mysteries and thrillers—the largest genre behind romances, which tend to be published more uniformly throughout the year—make up 20% to 47% of the total. "Leading Book Genres in the U.S. 2015." Statista. Oct. 7, 2015. https://www.statista.com/statistics/201404/types-of-books-that-american-adults-read; Franks, R. "A Taste for Murder: The Curious Case of Crime Fiction." *Journal of Media and Culture*, 17:1 (2014). https://doi.org/10.5204/mcj.770; van Dam, Andrew. "Department of Data: How Many Books Did You Read in 2023?" *Washington Post*, Jan. 5, 2024. www.washingtonpost.com/business/2024/01/05/how-many-books-did-you-read-2023-see-how-you-stack-up

15—A few examples: https://artsandculture.google.com/story/hidden-details-in-4-famous-paintings

16—Lessing, Lawrence. "Great American Scientists: The Chemists." *Fortune*, April 1960, pp. 131-134

17—Acar, Oguz A., et al. "Creativity and Innovation Under Constraints: A Cross-Disciplinary Integrative Review." *Journal of Management*, 45:1, Jan. 2019, pp. 96–121, https://doi.org/10.1177/0149206318805832

18—Meade, Michael. *Fate and Destiny: The Two Agreements of the Soul*. Massachusetts: Green Fire Press, 2010, p. 209

19—For instance, see https://www.atlasobscura.com/articles/headstones-that-defied-expectations

Embrace Winter's Wisdom

Lovers of winter are known as chionophiles. They're a small minority in most surveys, but they defend their affection by pointing to everything from snow sports and year-end holidays to fuzzy sweaters, hot drinks, and fireplaces.[1] These bring to mind the Danish concept of *hygge*, roughly translated as cozy, homey comfort. Its appeal seems obvious in a land that enjoys fewer than eight hours of wintertime daylight.

Wherever you live, the relatively chilly darkness of winter is a feature, not a bug. If sunlight and warmth flowed year-round as in summer, plants and animals would be tempted to keep working at full speed. Even in the tropics, many don't. On a recent winter trip to Hawaii, I enjoyed the odd, bare sticks of plumeria trees that had lost both flowers and leaves in their seasonal dormancy. These trees have the wisdom to rest.

Humans, enchanted by electricity, tend to forget nature has reasons for darkness and inhospitable weather. We often see winter's gloom as an annoyance rather than a reminder to slow down and rest. But humans need rest—often desperately in today's world. Extensive research demonstrates that insufficient rest makes workers less productive, more prone to errors, and less creative than if they'd simply taken time off.[2] Winter gives us an assigned time to recharge.

But rest does not imply that nothing is happening. Hibernating mama bears are growing new cubs in their wombs as they snore. Plants are stashing nutrients and extending their roots to prepare for spring growth. It's just that winter activities may be less obvious because the season presses us toward both physical and psychological interiors.

Winter energies in brief: *Rest, reflection, vision, illusion and magic, preparation, and communal endurance through hard times until plans can be enacted.*

First, we typically need physical shelter against harsh weather, and challenging conditions historically required people to work together to ensure survival. As a result, the season draws attention to relationships and mutual dependence. Accordingly, shelter is as much a state of mind as a roof. The concept embraces psychological baggage related to safety, identity, memory, culture, and control. Literally and figuratively, winter is a time to attend what shelters you as an artist, where and with whom you feel at home, and what gives you refuge against rejection or perceived failures.

In addition, winters are prime time for what goes on inside our heads—our thoughts, hopes, imaginings, and other mental activity. It's the season of Sages. More darkness also implies more time with our dreams—as well as the performance of dreams scripted by others. That's why performing arts venues and galleries tend to be more active in winter.

In that spirit, the sense most associated with winter is vision. This may seem counterintuitive in winter's darkness, blinding blizzards, and blankets of snow. But it's mental, *inner* vision that winter prompts—like the hallucinations caused by sensory deprivation,[3] sometimes known as "prisoner's cinema." That makes winter ideal for dreaming up stories, revisioning old ones, and planning for the future.

The activities in this section will help you engage in such visions, rest, get more rooted, and persevere. Let seasonal sensations of cold and damp remind you of these intentions as you prepare to bring wintertime dreams to life as the seasons cycle again toward spring.

How to put winter energy to work

▶ **Rest and prepare for the future:** Winter is the ideal time to work on your creative process rather than creative products. That's not to say you can't continue productive work. But winter resonates with turning inside, recuperating, and using realizations gleaned from autumn reflections to plan ways to

The season presses us toward interiors, both physical and psychological.

work smarter. Related activities in this section include Gnaw Your Creative Bone (p. 168) and Rest with the Rain (p. 178). In particular, for January 1, consider skipping resolutions (most of which are soon abandoned) and instead Take Stock with a Snowflake (p. 165) or Build a Better Vision Board (p. 189).

▶ **Grow stronger roots:** The bare winter limbs of many plants are a phase, not a failing. Their roots absorb nutrients even in winter and may grow when conditions allow, invisibly preparing for strong growth above ground in spring.[4] Try to apply the same understanding to any fallow time of your own, with faith it will pass. Consider using it to build a stronger practice and support system. Tend your creative roots with the activities called Picture This (p. 163), Strengthen Roots by Mining Memories (p. 175), Find Shelter (but Avoid Cages) (p. 173), and Expose Something Hiding (p. 170).

▶ **Entertain dreams, illusions, storytelling, and magic:** Countless generations huddled around winter fires telling stories. That may be one reason winter is associated with old age; stories are cultural memories told by the elders to pass along community wisdom. Long winter nights also give us more time to tell ourselves stories through dreams. Many of those stories feature Otherworlds, the imaginal or spirit worlds embraced by nearly every human culture.[5] Even scientists recognize a modern Otherworld known as the subconscious, where creativity gestates.

The sense most associated with winter is vision—especially inner vision and dreams.

Winter's reminders of death connect it to such Otherworlds, including the underworld where Greek Persephone spends her winters with Hades. These influences make supernatural events, shapeshifting, and other magic native to winter. Magicians, so potent or even monstrous in liminal autumn, are more likely to be cuddly in winter. (Think of singing snowmen or a certain oversized elf.) To explore their wintertime Otherworlds, check out the activities called Step into a Story (p. 182), Sidle up to Storytellers (p. 186), or Fracture Your Own Fairy Tale (p. 195). This is also a great time explore dreams. Dreamwork is beyond the scope of this book (and don't waste your time with "interpretation" dictionaries), but joining a class or dream group can be productive and fun for creatives.

▶ **Endure with help from others:** Although modern winters are easier to survive than they once were, short, gloomy days can be daunting. Winter is when archetypical Rulers and Sages lead us through difficult times, so use this season to strengthen ties to your creative community and recover or build strength for the future. Persist. That may mean knuckling down with hard work between bouts of rest. Recognize the difference between rest and procrastination (you know) and ignore temptations to quit. See the activities called Shine Light on Deceptions (p. 192), Acknowledge Loss (p. 184), and Practice Resilience with Rocks (p. 180).

> *Use this season to strengthen ties with your creative community, and recover or build strength for the future. Persist.*

"When your doors are shut and your room is dark, you are not alone. The will of nature is within you as your natural genius is within. Listen to its importuning. Follow its directives."
—*Greek Stoic philosopher Epictetus*

Winter activities that follow:

Picture This	163
Take Stock with a Snowflake	165
Gnaw Your Creative Bone	168
Expose Something Hiding	170
Find Shelter (but Avoid Cages)	173
Strengthen Roots by Mining Memories	175
Rest with the Rain	178
Practice Resilience with Rocks	180
Step into a Story	182
Acknowledge Loss	184
Sidle up to Storytellers	186
Build a Better Vision Board	189
Shine Light on Deceptions	192
Fracture Your Own Fairy Tale	195

Picture This

How this can help you: Expand your ability to see, create, and communicate meaning by converting emotions or abstract ideas into visual images.

Shortly after a shattering loss, I stumbled on photography as a way to both express my grief and create a merciful distance from it. Finding images that fit a specific, related theme such as memory, pain, or absence engaged my creativity in my own recovery and helped me transcend the emotions without evading them. Over time, I realized the effort was also sharpening my awareness of symbol, metaphor, analogy, and even the subtle meanings we frequently assign to colors, various types of lighting, and shapes.

Feeling as though I'd learned a new way to see, I expanded the practice to different moods and more abstract ideas. Rather than aiming for beautiful photos or results worth sharing, it focuses on stripping complex images or ideas to essentials.

Why this activity fits winter: *It draws on winter's associations with visuals, the intellect, and reduction to a bare essence.*

This activity is most effective when repeated over time, in different environments or as a regular practice. (It fits spring almost as well as winter because it gives ideas more tangible form, like a bare stem unfurling a leaf.) It's also fun in small groups, where you can learn from the symbolic thinking of others.

Picture This—Step by Step

You'll need: Your phone or other camera and at least 20 minutes. I recommend taking more time, repeating the activity regularly with different subjects, or both.

1. **Create a list of at least four abstract words related to a current project.** These might be thematic words, moods, or character traits, for instance. See the list below for ideas. Alternately, choose at least four of the following. Take a snapshot of your list to refer to.

☐ Connection	☐ Pain	☐ Emptiness
☐ Action	☐ Stillness	☐ Beginning
☐ Endurance	☐ Hope	☐ Comfort
☐ Preparation	☐ Anger	☐ Brilliance
☐ Conflict	☐ Humor	☐ Time
☐ Wisdom	☐ Persistence	☐ Promise

Wildly Inspired

2. **Find something to photograph**, indoors or out, that evokes or exemplifies each of your chosen subjects. Think more symbolically than literally. Other tips:
    + Consider different angles or get much closer than usual.
    + Arrange or interfere with your subject as need be or challenge yourself to shoot subjects strictly as you find them.
    + Experiment with blurring, poor lighting, black and white only, or overexposure.
    + Play with your phone camera's more obscure editing effects to see if any of those impart their own meanings.
    + Finding a striking image and assigning it an emotion or idea, rather than the other way around, is not cheating.
3. Juxtaposition (one thing next to another or in sequence) is an especially powerful way to create meaning. **Put one to three of your images together** (or take another that will work with one you already have) to create a visual story. Or use a few images as a prompt and write a paragraph, poem, or short story about them.
4. If you enjoy social media, **post one of your images** with its meaning to you and ask others to react or share different meanings they take from it instead.

My images for "despair" (above) and "hope" (right).

Take Stock with a Snowflake

How this can help you: Gaining clarity on where you are now—including any half-conscious insights or misperceptions—can help you more effectively plan your next steps.

If there's a bright side to the implied death of winter, it's the opportunity to turn away from past disappointments and start fresh. A pristine blanket of snow clears space for new possibilities, if not quite the same way a rising sun does. New Year's Resolutions and the selection of guiding words for the year capitalize on this "out with the old" energy.

There's an often-overlooked step between the past and the future, however—*now*. You might know where you want to go, but a map is less helpful if you're unsure of your current location. We need that "you are here" dot! Similarly, it's useful to understand where you are today, consciously and unconsciously, before moving ahead.

Why this activity fits winter: *It draws on winter's associations with visualization, especially visions that emerge from within, and preparation for the future.*

That doesn't mean looking backward. (If you feel the need to shake off the past, however, turn to Release What's No Longer Useful on p. 131 before completing this activity.) Rather, it requires investigating your present position. This fun way to do it begins with a short, guided meditation that will help you remember just how far you've come. Then it uses techniques from mandala psychology and Peter Levitt's *Fingerpainting on the Moon* to mine your subconscious for current fears or preoccupations. Greater awareness of those can help you remove internal blocks and move forward.

Take Stock with a Snowflake—Step by Step

You'll need: A journal or paper, a pen, about 45 minutes, and an Internet connection to access the recorded meditation at https://youtu.be/UoIeENv-19k, which is about 7 minutes long.

1. **Ready your materials and workspace.** Consider lighting a candle or working only by light shining from another room. If you don't want to write in this book, copy or trace the snowflake diagram on the next page. Include the dashed and dotted lines, perhaps in pencil or a second color.
2. Get comfortable and **listen to the meditation** at https://youtu.be/UoIeENv-19k.
3. When you reach the end of the meditation, **look at the snowflake** on the next page (or your copy). Notice the little circle at the tip of each long arm. Starting at the top, stare at that circle as if it were a tiny window into the room that is your Now. Imagine one letter of

Wildly Inspired

the alphabet emerging there as if approaching you through a blizzard. Try not to "decide" on a letter; let one arise by itself. Write it in the circle.

4. **Move clockwise to the next tip** and let a letter emerge there, too. Repeat until you've got six letters, one in each circle.

5. Now **look again at the top and the first letter** that emerged for you. With your creative work in mind, let a word that starts with that letter spring into your thoughts. Write it alongside the tip of the snowflake. (So if the letter is G, that word might be Group, Greedy, or Go, for instance.) Again, try to let it emerge rather than making a conscious decision. Repeat until you've written a word for each letter.

6. **Answer these questions about your words** in a journal:
   - What are your initial reactions to these words? Are there any surprises?
   - Is there a theme?
   - Which pairs, if any, represent opposites or synonyms?
   - Which words strike you as positive, negative, or neutral?

- Which words are about the work itself? Which are about your process, creative identity, community?
- Are any of the words about other aspects of your life, rather than your work? If so, why? How do those life concerns impact your work?

7. **Notice the dashed horizontal line** through the middle of the snowflake, which leaves three words above the line and three below. Does either set of three have anything in common?
    + Especially note the three below that dashed line, which can represent ideas that have emerged from below our ordinary consciousness. In that light, how might any one of those three (or all of them together) reflect a truth you've avoided or been unaware of?

8. Next, consider the dotted triangles behind the snowflake, one pointing upward and one pointing downward. Upward-pointed and downward-pointed triangles, alone and together, are highly symbolic across human cultures and over time.[6] **Look at the three words at the points of the triangle pointing upward**, which frequently represents spirit or intellect or goals, as well as fire and masculine energies. What have your "upward" three words got to do with those meanings or each other?

9. Also **consider the three words at the points of the triangle pointing downward**, which often represent physical or practical matters or blockages, as well as water, earth, and feminine energies. What have the three words on that triangle got to do with those ideas or each other?

10. **Choose one word from your triangle, or one answer to the questions above**, that strikes you as meaningful or important to you now. Journal about it for 5 minutes. How can this insight help you move forward in the coming year?

Gnaw Your Creative Bone

 *How this can help you:* Clarify your motivations to help you prioritize and add authenticity to your work while making it more personally satisfying.

Winter is a time of bones—the newly visible bones of deciduous trees, the bone-white skies before snow, and the bones left for soup once food stores have dwindled. It's also a time for deep consideration of the spine of your creativity: why you do it and how it gives structure and meaning to your days. It's been my experience that most creatives have one or a few themes that their work explores again and again—artistic obsessions. I believe that kind of theme or obsession is what Henry David Thoreau[7] had in mind when he offered this advice:

Why this activity fits winter: *It draws on winter's associations with mental activity, community contributions, and reflection.*

> *"Pursue, keep up with, circle round and round your life, as a dog does his master's chaise. Do what you love. Know your own bone; gnaw at it, bury it, unearth it, gnaw it still."*

This activity encourages gnawing your bone to clarify the purpose of creativity in your life. Artistic mission statements have become popular in recent years, mostly as a component of branding. But understanding what drives your creative impulses is even more important for motivation, originality, and psychological growth—especially in lean times when commercial success seems evasive. What keeps you going? That's the marrow you need to sink your teeth into.

Gnaw Your Creative Bone—Step by Step

You'll need: A journal, a pen, and 30–45 minutes.

1. Curl up somewhere cozy, maybe next to a winter fire or within the scent of a bubbling soup, and **answer some or all of the following questions** for yourself:

   - "The way you do anything is the way you do everything." (And probably for the same reasons.) When you read this, what personal traits come to mind? How are they reflected in your creative work?
   - What in your childhood may have led you to these tendencies?
   - Name *two* of the earliest remembered or most formative books, movies, or other artistic experiences from your childhood. What do you recall about the situations in which you encountered them? (This might include who you were with, where you were, etc.) What do the two have in common, if anything?
   - Are there ways in which your own art retells, reflects, or contrasts with those two?

- If you're aware of a theme, conflict, question about life, or specific symbol that you can't leave alone in your work, what is it? Why might that be?
- How have friends, fellow creatives, instructors, or industry professionals described your work, style, or themes? (If it helps, contact someone and ask them.) Do you agree, disagree, or want to prove them wrong?
- What values do you most want your work (and your life) to express? List a half dozen or more.
- What inspires you?
- What unusual or formative experiences have you had that inform your work (or perhaps should)?
- When it comes to creativity, art, or story, what do you most fervently believe?
- What have you recently realized or no longer believe?
- Where on your priority list does creative time rank? (If you've already done it, refer to the Autumn activity called Examine Your Plate on p. 129. It might be more accurate than your instinctive answer.)
    - ☐ Right at the top ☐ In the top three ☐ In the top five
    - ☐ After _____ but before _____
    - ☐ After every other responsibility and chore, even the hated ones
    - ☐ Other: _____
- What do you do with old or abandoned projects? Where or how do you keep or dispose of them?
- What do your answers to the last two questions say about how much you respect your own work or consider it important, consciously or unconsciously?
- If you want to change those priorities, rituals, or attitudes, what's one step you could take?
- If your life is a long-term art project, how is that creation going? What's missing right now that you can take steps to add?

2. **Create or update a personal artist's manifesto**, using any parts of the pattern below you find helpful. This statement can be useful in personal branding and marketing, but it's intended more to hearten and motivate you.

> I draw on *[core values, inspirations, or experiences]* to create *[what kinds of work]* for *[who, specifically]*.
>
> I do this because *[why you care or what you believe]*.
>
> I refuse to *[self-doubts, outdated beliefs, bad attitudes, or other things that might hold you back]*.
>
> No matter the outcome, I'll keep doing what I do because *[how this work is a part of who you are]*.

3. **Post your statement somewhere you can see it** frequently but not so often it becomes invisible.

4. Since this kind of thinking tends to work in your mind on time-delay, **pay attention to dreams or thoughts about this activity** that bubble into your mind over the next few days. Perhaps they can illuminate or should modify the work you've done here.

Expose Something Hiding

 *How this can help you:* Raise your awareness of half-conscious hopes, fears, and concerns and strengthen your ability to tap your intuition.

While autumn reveals, winter often hides things again. Snow or moldering leaves obscure trails and yards. Ashen clouds conceal blue skies for days at a time, sometimes challenging our faith that a sun still shines beyond. And the season kicks off with holiday gifts hidden in wrappings.

But winter's efforts to hide are imperfect. The same snow that hides grass announces the passage of unseen creatures through their tracks. Fresh molehills may erupt overtop to remind us of life under the surface.

Why this activity fits winter: *It aligns with the season's focus on visuals, both seen and unseen.*

One morning, only days after a wintertime move to the Midwest, I called my dogs for their breakfast. One, perpetually hungry, bounded through the dog door from outside. The other didn't. He'd already escaped through our fence once, leaving me searching for days before a neighbor corralled him. Now snow lay knee-deep, the temperatures below zero. I imagined him frozen stiff under a bush or loping across seven states toward the home we'd left behind. I ran barefoot into the snow, calling his name.

No response. Even the snow lay mute: No paw prints pointed out which way he'd gone. I'd uprooted him to create a new life, and already it'd veered into disaster.

Wait—was that movement in my peripheral vision?

I spun. A muzzle thrust up from a snowbank. A nose twitched, then my yellow-eyed dog erupted. Snow flew. He must have come outside during the night and, insulated by his thick undercoat, fallen asleep as snow mounted until he wasn't even a lump in the drift.

Lazily he stretched and shook. As he tolerated my relieved hug, I made a mental note: Next time, put on shoes first. Clearly the notion he might freeze was silly. He'd only exposed my own hidden fears about the change I'd imposed on our lives.

Exposing such feelings is the first step to dealing with them. This activity, which is based on a psychotherapy tool, can uncover hidden concerns or nascent ideas, thus helping you create with more insight and heart.[8] I've done more involved versions with craft supplies and glue, and a clever artist friend adds a dimension of time by creating the initial squiggle over several pages to launch a story. The simple approach here works as well for most people, though. It's especially fun with a creative friend (including a child).

Embrace Winter's Wisdom

Expose Something Hiding—Step by Step

You'll need: A good-sized sheet of paper (a drawing pad or 11" x 17" size is best); one or more felt pens, crayons, or pastels; and 20–30 minutes.

1. Optional: If you're struggling with anything particular in your creative life, distill it down to a few words such as "stuck" or "what next?" **Scrawl that word or phrase, large and messily, on the paper,** perhaps without ever lifting your pen. Then turn the paper 90 degrees. Alternately, just hold your concern in mind. If things are going great, start with Step 2.

2. **First, loosen up by moving your arms—wiggling, flopping, or in circles.** Research says this is an important step,[9] so don't skip it!

3. Keeping your pen on the page the whole time, **add a substantial squiggle or scribble right overtop.** Don't stop too soon. These tips can help:
    + **If you're alone**, close your eyes, and draw your squiggle over anything written in Step 1. Keep going until it feels like your hand has moved enough.
    + **If you're doing this with a friend**, swap papers, rotate 90 degrees from any writing, close your eyes, and draw a squiggle or scribble on the other person's paper, again continuing until if feels like you've done enough. Then give it back to the original owner.
    + **If you feel tense or self-conscious**, try using your nondominant hand instead.

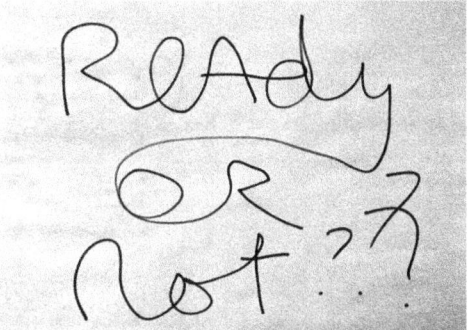 

4. **Look for images that begin to emerge** as if you were finding shapes in clouds. Turn the page in all directions and use your imagination. If nothing jumps out, try looking from farther away or in a mirror.

5. Changing pen colors if you like, **add to, fill in, or outline parts of the squiggle to turn it into a few images (or words).** Notice your feelings as you do this. If refining one image overwrites or messes up another, choose which is more important, or use different colors to keep both. If you don't see any images, think less literally or elaborate on

Wildly Inspired

existing lines and shapes to draw whatever first comes to mind. Feel free to label images or add thoughts as you work.

6. **Consider or journal on these questions**:
   - If you did Step 1, how might one of these images answer or address your original concern?
   - What were your reactions during Step 5? Were you excited, confused, intrigued, disappointed? Why?
   - If an image feels threatening or disturbing, what uncomfortable truth or fear might you be avoiding?
   - Alternately, if you feel "meh" about what was revealed, ask yourself what you wish had appeared and why. Like tossing a coin to make a decision and getting the "wrong" side of the coin, this question can reveal what you didn't realize you wanted. Or your reaction might hint at too much focus on end results or reluctance to occasionally make the kind of mess that can spark innovation.

   For instance, in the example at left, I first saw a pregnant woman, a person or angel with wings, a dragonfly, and a bassinette, along with some flames, an open clam, and a couple of boomerangs, one of which I turned into a crooked smile instead. The themes of birth and flight jump out, which I think answers my "ready or not?" question, while the angel watching over reassures me.

   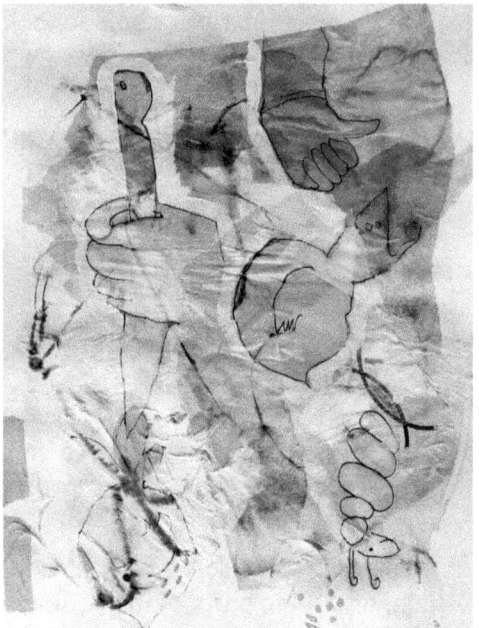

   In a variation on this activity that uses tissue paper and glue as well as squiggles (right), I first saw and outlined a quail, a second bird that could also be a lemon, a caterpillar, a hand clutching a knife, and a thumb's-up. The knife concerned me—did my work need to be cut? Or was I gripping something so tightly it was going to cause pain? Then I realized the knife could be stabbing the lemon to make lemonade. That resonated more for me, since the thumb's up suggested I was on the right track, and the caterpillar promised a butterfly to come. I see other shapes today I didn't originally notice—because I'm in a different mental place—and might interpret the original images differently, too. (For instance, is the quail actually a chicken, especially given "quail" as a verb? The answer is up to the artist!)

7. **Identify a way to act on your insights**, whether it's as simple as proceeding with more confidence or you'd like to further explore a particular image or feeling, for instance.

Find Shelter (but Avoid Cages)

How this can help you: Gain insight into the varieties and meanings of shelter so you can use the inherent conflicts to make your work more universal.

In winter, our worlds subtly shrink. We take shelter, withdrawing into our homes, cars, and thicker clothing. Especially in challenging or uncertain times, we fall back on routines and well-worn habits—psychological shelter that help create emotional security.

Whether physical or psychological, these layers of protection keep us more comfortable, at least for a while. But they can also be restrictive, isolating, or deceptive. I often walk through the winter woods during rain. Although fir, cedar, and hemlock boughs catch most of the showers, I stay dry only until wind tosses the trees. Then the rain in the branches drops in great, startling splats. I end at least as wet and with nerves on edge, too. All shelters, not just trees, have a dark side.

Why this activity fits winter: *It draws on winter's nudge to find refuge and turn within before eventually launching outward again.*

In fact, a hero's journey depends on the hero being lured (or dragged) from shelter into a dangerous world of new experiences—because what starts as a shelter can turn into a cage. Consider the janitorial closet where the protagonist of Laurie Halse Anderson's novel *Speak* hides and heals from a trauma. At the climax of the story, that safe space is ruptured, but that catalyst allows Melinda to break free from what has inadvertently become a prison.[10]

The right balance between protection and limitation can be a powerful source of art, conflict, and story. Use this activity to explore the tension between security and growth for your creativity, for a character, or both.

Find Shelter—Step by Step

You'll need: A pen, a journal, and 30–45 minutes (or more if you do Step 1).

1. (Optional but encouraged.) Take a short walk outside to **notice different types of shelter.** These might range from a hollow tree to a caterpillar's cocoon. (If the weather's too crummy, use your imagination or images online.) Try to find at least four kinds of shelters.

    + Notice how a shelter good at one kind of protection may be poor protection from a different kind of threat. *(For instance, a bird's nest is beyond the reach of prowling cats but may be at risk from a strong wind or a hungry hawk.)*

- + If you can find one, turn over a big rock or log to see if anything lives beneath. Consider how one creature's shelter might be a crushing weight on another.
2. Once you can conveniently write, **answer the following questions** for yourself or your character in your journal:
    - What does "shelter" mean to you? Consider physical shelters, all the hazards that someone may need shelter from, and psychological or emotional shelters, such as reading a book to escape from daily concerns.
    - What are three types of physical shelter you've experienced? How did each make you feel? What was a weakness of each?
    - What are three types of psychological shelters you've experienced? What did each protect you from? What limitations did each create?
    - What or who do *you* shelter, and how does that role drain or empower you or affect your own sense of security?
    - What or who shelters or protects you *as an artist*—psychologically, financially, or otherwise? *(A few examples: a mentor, a babysitter who gives you more time, past success, your creative community.)*
        - What is it or they protecting you from? How sufficient is that protection?
        - How might that security also constrain you?
        - How could you strengthen your protection while rejecting or escaping its limits?
3. **Identify a way to incorporate your insights** into your creative practice or a project. *That might mean finding more psychic shelter to increase your artistic confidence or pushing yourself out of a haven that's become limiting. Or it might involve simply adding meaningful details to a shelter depicted in your work.*
4. *Storytellers:* **Answer these additional questions for a project:**
    - How, when, or why did the character get into their current shelter situation?
    - What, if anything, identifies their shelter as their own? *(Decorations, a secret location…)*
    - In what way could (or does) that shelter leak, give way, or otherwise fail them?
    - Which is more of a driving need for your character: Finding more or better protection, or struggling against shelter they've outgrown or is too confining?
    - How does that need affect their identity or actions? *(For instance, one confined child might rebel, but another might try harder to please.)* In what ways are you, the creator, sheltering your character, and from what? In other words, what is one way you could make them feel less safe as they work toward their goal? Doing so can add conflict and tension to the story.
5. *Storytellers:* **Write one of the following scenes:**
    - ☐ Your character either loses a shelter they expect to rely on or finds an unexpected form of shelter.
    - ☐ The character's familiar shelter remains intact, but their expectations for it (physical or psychological) are defied in a way that shocks them.
    - ☐ The character expresses their need to find better protection or their frustration about being overprotected.

Strengthen Roots by Mining Memories

How this can help you: Draw on personal and family memories as fodder for creative work—and strengthen those emotional roots in the process.

One of my most personal manuscripts—and a lot of life insight—began as a startling question asked by the leader of an afternoon writing workshop. We'd already worked through several routine prompts, writing about first kisses and first trouble at school. But a different question unlocked more treasure for me: What *don't* you remember, and why not? This inquiry forced me to rifle my memories for something missing that, as an adult, I knew intellectually should be there. It plunged me deeper into the corners of memories I could reach and helped me understand more about my own quirks and passions. It also sent me searching for equally unusual prompts that, at least for me, more reliably provide access to bone-deep emotion than mundane, "classic" prompts.

Why this activity fits winter: *It aligns with winter's focus on mental activity, internal vision, and the strengthening of hidden roots.*

Memories form the roots of who you are now. Plunging into a few you might not often revisit may provide ideas for specific creative work you'd like to pursue. More importantly, the emotions stored in those memories like sap can be transferred to a current project. They'll provide emotional authenticity (despite differences in the specific situations) and help support creative growth in the future.

One caution: Take care with accessing any long-ago traumas you haven't worked through with a qualified professional. You know your own tolerances and can stop any time.

Mine Memories—Step by Step

You'll need: A journal and pen and 5 minutes or more per question. This is a good activity to muse during walks, chores, or similar repetitive activities, and then take up the writing later.

1. In a journal, **answer the following questions** for yourself. Choose those that appeal—although any that provoke a negative reaction may be the richest veins to tap. You might want to tackle the list one at a time over days or weeks. You may also want to save some answers for family—or not!
   - What is your absolute earliest memory? What emotions made that memory stick in your young brain? Can you also identify the next two or three? What emotions, sensations, themes, or people do they have in common?
   - What's one thing you did in your childhood that you shouldn't have or that you felt then or feel now was out of character? (It may have been harmful to someone or forbidden,

or it may have simply been a strange impulse.) How did it make you feel then, and why? In what ways do you see it differently now?
- Consider the best thing that ever happened to you. What was the first challenging or difficult thing to occur *after* the good one? How were the two related, if at all? How did the good thing influence your reaction to or memories of the bad one, or vice versa?
- Consider the worst thing that ever happened to you. What happened right *before* that? How were the two related, if at all? Write about that pre-disaster time, event, or feeling.
- If you could click a button to permanently forget one painful memory, which would it be, and why that one? What hidden (if painful) gifts or lessons from that memory might make you hesitate over the button?
- What *don't* you remember from your life? Why not? What else was going on or discouraged you from remembering? Ways to access this challenging set of questions include:
  + Reflect on family stories or jokes about you, or photos that include you, and that you've heard or seen many times but in truth have no personal memory of, at least on the surface. Try to separate the family legend from your personal recall. What else may have been happening to distract you, or why didn't you have the kind of emotional reaction that sealed the incident in others' memories? Can you identify deviations from the legend that might be closer to the truth from your viewpoint?
  + Think about lighthearted "firsts" you must have experienced that may not have been emotional enough to leave a mark. These might include your first pair of socks, the first time you were allowed to dress yourself how you wanted, or a first encounter with a new person, pet, or favorite food.
  + Consider "firsts" that are potentially more traumatic than the usual happy ones: the first time somebody hit you, first argument or punishment, first hospitalization, first car accident, first time you realized a parent was wrong or human. Start a list and pick one to explore more deeply.
  + Spend time with the "why not?" part of the question alone. What was the general atmosphere of your childhood? What whirled around you, positive or negative? What conditions may have made it difficult for any one incident to stand out? What were you so focused on that everything else fell away? Does this thinking summon any shred of memory you'd like to explore?
- How can you use any memories you dug up—or their absence—in your work?

2. **Find something in the land around you that's old**: A rock bluff, a tree, a visible fossil, a body of water more established than a puddle, for instance. Imagine you have access to the memory of the land. What has your elder thing witnessed? What memory can you invent for it—and what in your own memories prompted your imagination to jump there?

3. **Select a minor aspect of your home's décor** that you personally chose, from a houseplant to a kitchen implement. Reach back into your memory to an early experience with such a thing. (There was undoubtedly a model or instance of it in your life that made you believe you needed one, too, as you created your own sense of home.) What happened regarding that item to give it an emotional aura for you?

4. **Identify an object that's important or sentimental** for you. What is *this object's* most important or favorite memory? (It may not be the one most significant to you.) Use your own memories or your imagination as much as you like.
5. If you've answered several of these questions, **what patterns emerge?** Are there consistent emotions, images, or people involved?
6. Identify at least one thing you've recalled—from an emotion or motivation to a sensory detail—and **incorporate it into a project** to add authenticity.
7. *Storytellers:* **Deepen character and plot** by knowing the answers to these questions:
   - What is your main character's earliest memory? Why that one?
   - What does that character know about their own "origin story"—how or where they were born, how they were named, or what role they took in their family? What parts of that story may be false or still hidden?
   - What early experience created or reinforced your character's biggest strength?
   - What early experience prompted or shaped the character's flaws, failings, or misunderstandings about life?
   - What does the character most wish they could forget, and why? How does this pain or regret influence their present actions or the story?
   - Identify one physical item your character always has with them or otherwise finds indispensable (from an item of jewelry to a weapon)—even if it doesn't play a role in your story. What memory of their first or an early encounter with it gives it such significance?
   - What important memory belongs not to a character but to an object or location in your story? How does this memory influence the present?
   - What key memory motivates an antagonist in the story?

Rest with the Rain

 *How this can help you:* Raise your awareness of ways to recharge your creativity by making rest a higher priority.

Not everything in nature takes time off during winter, but from wood frogs whose hearts stop to flower bulbs that need cold dormancy before they can sprout, most life slows or withdraws to conserve energy until spring.[11] Modern human culture resists this natural cycle, but whether we're talking about soil, athletic performance, or creativity, relentless productivity leads to exhaustion. Too little rest will stunt future growth.

Why this activity fits winter: *It encourages taking a similar fallow period for yourself.*

Fortunately, winter weather nudges us to accept, if not plan, for creative rest. Sparkling sunshine on snow draws us outside to play, but rain, ice, and biting cold aren't nearly as fun. Most people retreat from winter weather, making the season more restful, at least potentially. (Shoveling out driveways excepted.) This activity, which may look deceptively simple, can enforce at least one quiet time to help refill your creative well.

Rest with the Rain—Step by Step

You'll need: A journal, a pen, a timer, and about 20 minutes. A hot beverage is optional.

1. On a rainy, frosty, or blustery day when you can work a short time without being disturbed, **sit near a window**, perhaps with a hot beverage.
2. Open your journal to a full spread. **Label the left-hand page "Parking Lot."**
3. Set a timer for 15 minutes, then sit and do nothing but **attend the sights and sounds outside** for the entire time as you proceed with the steps below. (This can be surprisingly difficult.) Breathe deeply. Aim to only observe and rest.
4. Every time you think of something other than the weather—tasks you "ought" to be doing, things to remember, problems you've mused—**jot a note** in the Parking Lot and let them go until later. Put your attention back onto Step 5.
5. The rest of the time, **answer these questions** on the right-hand page of your journal or other pages as needed:
   - What do you notice outside your window—sights, sounds, scents, and any tactile sensations you can infer? *(Raindrops hitting the glass and the smell of moldering leaves, for instance.)*
   - What related sensations surface, either now or from past experience? *(The feeling of being damp and then getting warm and dry is one example.)*

- What images or metaphors does your view prompt? *(For instance, I watched rain drip off my porch in rows of droplets that put me in mind of a music box cylinder or player piano scroll.)*
- What emotions or memories do these weather sensations evoke for you?
- What changes over your 15 minutes of observation (including in your own body or mind)?

6. When the timer goes off, **circle any answers that might find a place in your work**. But even if you wrote little, you'll probably find yourself more relaxed and ready to go on with your day.

7. **Before taking care of anything in the Parking Lot,** consider trying one of these restful options each week all winter to help your creativity thrive.

    ☐ Soak up stories in any form. Instead of a campfire, most of us today gather around the glow of a screen or reading lamp, but the impulse is the same. Put dark evenings to use by transporting yourself into favorite genres or new ones.

    ☐ Occasionally turn off the podcast, audio book, music, or—especially—news. Spend time in silence and let your mind wander. You'll better hear inner wisdom about creative decisions to be made or a change in direction. If you constantly drown out your internal voice, it'll stop.

    ☐ Take a 7-day or 24-hour social media blackout. (You won't miss anything that won't still be there when you return, I promise.) Admire how much more time and mental peace you have without it.

    ☐ Intentionally jettison (or postpone) a few things on your to-do list. You'll probably be pleasantly surprised how little difference it makes to anyone.

    ☐ Conversely, tackle a chore that's been nagging at you, such as prepping for taxes or cleaning out the car. The mental weight of such annoyances is often far greater than the effort to simply get them done.

    ☐ If you enjoy yoga, try an extended savasana such as the one I guide at https://youtu.be/tCFpfLHBe9o.

    ☐ Identify one thing you can do to give yourself a more restful physical space. Enlist help from family if needed. *(For instance, take 20 minutes to reduce clutter. Ideally, prevent it from building up again.)*

    ☐ Figure out how to manage another 30 minutes of sleep once a week. *(Ignore a favorite TV show to binge-watch it later, for example, or skip one morning shower a week if no one will know the difference anyway.)*

    ☐ Take yourself on an artist's date—as popularized by Julia Cameron's *The Artist's Way*. This might mean a museum trip (many have virtual exhibits and catalogues), a craft store, a session with finger paints, or any of a thousand other activities that might stimulate your aesthetic and physical senses. If you're new to the concept, find resources by Googling.

    ☐ Take the concept of the artist's date one step further by cross-training. What even mildly creative pursuit, separate from your work, has been calling you? Easy examples might be decorating cookies, a woodwork project, or calligraphy. Dip your toes in to replenish your inner artist.

Practice Resilience with Rocks

 *How this can help you:* Engage your imagination to find new ways of seeing and handling problems to surmount a challenge or get yourself out of a rut.

Although winter can bring hardships and loss, it also highlights resilience—often with a sassy spirit. Snow too deep to walk? Strap boards on your feet and glide. Life gone dormant? Create a playmate made of snow. Too dark to see? Study stars, stories, or dreams.

The spirit of wintertime resilience is to acknowledge barriers, but instead of dwelling on them, think sideways to find a different perspective and a playful way around (or at least amuse yourself until conditions change with time, as they always do). This is a skill you can hone to get through hard times of creative rejection or block.

Why this activity fits winter: *It aligns with the winter theme of endurance and creative getting-by.*

For instance, whenever I'm discouraged, I walk among tall trees that cling to cliffs. Their roots not only range widely over the boulders to find moisture and soil but burrow into the stone to eventually split it. The trees' method of overcoming obstacles and forging a secure place for themselves reminds me that patient, incremental growth can break through what appear to be impenetrable barriers.

Other aspects of nature use other approaches. How does a cloud or boulder solve challenges, and could those methods work for you? If so, what might that look like in your life or creative practice? Explore the answers with this activity.

Practice Resilience with Rocks—Step by Step

You'll need: Nothing but a journal, a pen, your imagination, and 20–30 minutes.

1. **Identify at least three natural elements that are evident in winter** and appeal to you or you're curious to know more about. Or do this activity from the perspective of a character and choose items that might interest them.
2. **For each item, consider and answer the questions below.** Stretch your imagination and see the examples for ideas. Going outside to study your choices with a fresh eye is optional but recommended—or, if you like, do some Internet research about them for inspiration.
   - How does this thing respond to physical barriers or other threats? *(For instance, a tumbling rock will crush obstacles or bounce off unharmed. A tree sends roots around or deeper below boulders or slowly, patiently splits them over time.)*

- What eats or otherwise might destroy this thing? How does it escape or defy those forces? *(For instance, earthworms avoid birds by staying deep in the dark, noting vibrations, and sometimes going into a dormancy akin to hibernation.)*
- How does this thing move, migrate, or change its form to survive? *(For instance, rivers take the path of least resistance, team up with other water to blast through barriers as floods, or change form to become glaciers that grind away obstacles.)*

3. **Identify a current project or creativity challenge—or the challenges facing your character—and brainstorm how each of nature's strategies might apply to that challenge.** Embrace silliness—if you (or the character) could solve the challenge without imagination, you already would have. New perspectives, even if a bit crazy, might jostle loose the idea or solution needed.

    For instance, a common creative challenge is "I can't find time to work on my art." The resilience of nature might solve that problem in these ways:

    + A rock takes the long perspective and may remain patiently inactive until its environment changes, freeing it to tumble, split, or become molten. Perhaps you can take a longer perspective, temporarily acknowledging other priorities and relaxing until the kids are older or other workloads ease.
    + A tree struggling for light leans toward clearings or focuses growth upward to rise above competing plants. Identify one direction you could lean toward a "clearing" of your time (rising earlier, doing creative work through lunch, or trying more intense but less time-consuming workouts, for instance). Or identify weedy competitors for your time that your creative work could overshadow for a while—such as by having groceries delivered instead of repeatedly shopping for them yourself.
    + A river that hits a barrier simply flows somewhere else. Try taking your creative tools out of the house (to a coffee shop or the soccer field sidelines?) to get flowing—or spill over into a different project for a while.

4. **Once you've come up with a few practical steps you could take, try them.** Learning what doesn't work can help reveal what will. Or, if you did this activity for a character, consider how one or more of the items they chose could be reflected in their personality, their name, or the story.

Step into a Story

 *How this can help you:* Increase awareness of the archetypes that inhabit stories while providing a mirror with which to see yourself or a character more clearly.

February 26 is National Tell a Fairy Tale Day in the United States, and some libraries—possibly inspired by National Library Lovers' Month—celebrate all month long.[12] Fairy tales have been with humans since at least the Bronze Age because they provide psychological models for dealing with change and hardship, choosing good over evil, and meeting the norms of the societies in which they're told.[13]

Why this activity fits winter: *It aligns with the season's focus on shared internal visions as a binder of community, legacy, and self-understanding.*

Psychology includes an entire subdiscipline related to the use of fairy tales and their archetypes in therapy. I've earned a certificate in this approach, so I'm confident in offering this activity as a fun way to explore a fairy or folk tale you identify with, not as therapy but to gain new perspectives on your own creative identity and how you might use fairy-tale archetypes in your work. Full explanations of the many ways to work with fairy tales fill other books, and this sample may whet your appetite for more. It relies on the Inuit tradition of Skeleton Woman, my personal favorite and ideal for winter. The story, which gained prominence in a retelling by Clarissa Pinkola Estés, has inspired several award-winning short films as well as less literal adaptations. Like all good fairy tales, it has multiple interpretations, including some that resonate well with issues in the lives of many creatives. Alternately, try this activity with a character in mind. You'll need to listen to or watch one of these recordings:

- A dreamy Irish short film at https://youtu.be/UJanCcIw03I, also found at https://englishroam.com/?p=26772
- Expert audio retellings at https://www.storymuseum.org.uk/1001-stories/skeleton-woman or a longer one in two halves (with a short recap) at https://www.youtube.com/watch?v=faQLfA467Cg. A last-ditch option, if none of the others remain available, is at https://www.youtube.com/watch?v=d5TACEJdk5I

Step into a Story—Step by Step

You'll need: A journal and pen, about 45 minutes, and Internet access to one of the story recordings listed above. The story is 12–20 minutes long, depending on the recording.

1. **Watch or listen to the story of Skeleton Woman** at any one of the links above.
2. **With the story in mind, answer these questions for yourself** (or your character) in your journal. You may not know the answers to some of the questions, but let them all steep inside you. Fairy tales work on a subconscious level.
   - Who or what is the punitive father character in your creative life (or your story)?
   - In what way do you (or the character) feel forgotten at the bottom of the sea?
   - What are you hungry or thirsty for?
   - What are you running away from based on mistaken assumptions?
   - What might you see if the running finally ends?
   - Who or what might help untangle the bones of your troubles?
   - What action or vulnerability in another might slake your hunger or thirst?
   - What surprising action (such as climbing into the fisherman's bed) could you take that might pivot you in an unexpected direction?
   - What is the beating heart of your life, your creativity, or your story?
   - How can you honor that heart to sing flesh back onto bones for a happy ending?
3. **Identify at least one way to incorporate your insights** into your creative practice or project.

Acknowledge Loss

How this can help you: Develop a character you're working with (including your own) and perhaps assess the value of creativity in your life.

None of us likes it, but there's no getting through life for long without loss. Winter tends to make this point, whether through houseplants that don't survive cooler temps or lost loved ones recalled during bittersweet holidays.

Loss, or the threat of it, is equally essential to creative work. Actions taken as a result of—or to avoid—a particular loss can drive the whole story. Many fairy tales are launched with the death of a parent, for instance. *The Wizard of Oz* never happens if Dorothy does not lose her home in the tornado, and the rebels in Star Wars must battle against not only the loss of their freedom to a repressive regime but the threat of the Death Star destroying their planets.

Why this activity fits winter: *It takes a clear look at hard times and how they shape us as we endure them.*

This activity, a modified version of a hospice empathy exercise, is a provocative tool for developing character desires, fears, and motivations. If you have the fortitude to also do it for yourself, it can be a reminder to prioritize time. We really can't know when misfortune might make the decisions too real.

Acknowledge Loss—Step by Step

You'll need: A dozen 3" x 5" cards, sticky notes, or similar slips of paper, a journal and pen, and at least 30 minutes.

1. Using one card or slip of paper for each, **write down your (or your character's):**
   + **Four most-prized material possessions.**
   + **Four most-loved activities.**
   + **Four most important people,** living, fictional, or dead. Don't group them as "family" or "kids"—individual names or relationships only. Yes, the limit is four. Whether you include pets in people or possessions is up to you.
2. Lay them all out so you can **appreciate these valued things all together.** Consider the following questions and note your thoughts in your journal:
   - Are there commonalities or themes?
   - How does the collection reflect or add up to your unique identity?
3. Life can be unlucky—but sometimes we still have choices. **Pick out two things you or the character must give up** and set those aside. Doing your best to imagine that loss really happening, answer these questions in your journal:

- What feelings or insights might you or the character have about those tough choices?
- How would the losses affect interactions with the important things that remain?

4. **Turn the remaining slips over so you can't see what's written and mix them around.**

5. Oh no! Disaster strikes randomly, too, and may come in waves. Without looking, **pick out three more you (or your character) are forced to lose.** In your journal, note:
   - What are they? How devastating is each loss?
   - What would be your or your character's likely reactions to each individually? *(Resignation, despair, flight, denial, anger/hostility, or clinginess, for instance?)*
   - How does any one of the losses affect your or the character's attitudes about the other losses? Does any one overshadow the rest, making the others unimportant? Or do they aggravate each other?
   - Do any of the losses make what's remaining more important—or suddenly unimportant? If so, which and why?

6. Turn the remaining items face up again. One loss often causes others, so **choose one more slip to let go of** and answer these questions in your journal:
   - How would this loss be easier or harder than the random, uncontrolled losses?

7. Look at the slips already lost. **What two items, activities, or people you or the character still enjoy would be worth sacrificing to get back one of those already lost?** (The trade doesn't have to be realistic.) If you want to make that trade, go ahead.
   - How does that decision feel? Is control better or worse than being subjected to fate?

8. Examine what's left and **choose two, and only two, worth literally any price or action to keep**. (Nobody wants to imagine this choice, but do it.) We'll call these the Top Two.

9. Celebrate that this is only a game and **answer these remaining questions** for yourself (or the character):
   - Are there any surprises in the Top Two? If every decision had been yours or the character's, which of the lost items would be in the Top Two instead?
   - If either of the Top Two were threatened next, what actions could you or the character conceivably take or justify to keep those things? Lies? Crime? Cruelty? Self-harm? Murder?
   - How does your character's initial story goal, or your creative work itself, relate to any or all of the full dozen items? Is there a way to make the connections stronger?
   - Did the initial dozen items include basics such as mobility, vision, or hearing? What (else) in your life or the character's is taken for granted but could be lost? Could any of those basics have a place in your work?
   - If you did this activity for yourself, are there ways to get more of the Top Two (or all 12) into every day of your life?

10. *Storytellers*: **Write a scene** in which one of your character's Top Two is realistically threatened and the only way to keep it will be to give up the other. What do they do? Alternately, write a scene in which your character has already suffered a Top Two loss and had some time to mourn. What action do they take next? How does the loss change their values, personality, or attitudes toward other people or the other things still in their life?

Sidle up to Storytellers

 *How this can help you:* Consider the stories you've heard or told yourself about creativity to eliminate unhelpful fictions or gain a new perspective on your own stories.

Winter is the season most associated with magic, whether fat red elves with flying reindeer, the wonder of frost patterns, or the promise of eternal life. In particular, it's the season for the magic of stories, whether told from personal and cultural memory, dreams, or pure invention. Our brains are wired to structure information into narrative form, and stories are a primary tool for giving our lives meaning.[14] Such meaning may never feel so important as during the season when death lurks just outside the door.

Why this activity fits winter: *It aligns with the season's focus on community, shared culture, and internal visions.*

As our tour guides to these magical realms, storytellers also hold a special place in the season—and often in our memories, too. My own favorite storyteller was a teacher, Miss Storch. All of perhaps 24 years old, she read fiction aloud each afternoon to fifth-graders who thought we were too old for such things. But our classroom was never so calm and attentive. She wasn't the first to encourage my writing, but she sparked inspiration better than most. Once I was published, I hoped to thank her. Unfortunately, my efforts to find her then failed.

This activity is here, in part, in her honor. It turns the spotlight from the stories to the tellers to examine any lingering influences, good or bad, on you, your work, or your characters. It provides a fresh framework through which to view your own stories.

Sidle up to Storytellers—Step by Step

You'll need: A source of flame (a hearth, woodstove, or candle), a journal and pen, and about 45 minutes. A recording device, such as your phone's voice memo app, is optional.

1. **Sit before a cozy fire or lit candle.** Gaze at the flame.
2. **Read this scene and imagine it** vividly. You might read one sentence and then close your eyes to imagine it before moving on to the next sentence. Or, record the entire scene for yourself so you can listen to the playback with your eyes closed.

    You're gazing into the flames of an ancient campfire at night and watching the flight of sparks into the dark. Hear the crackle of the fire. Smell the smoke. Feel heat where your body faces the fire... and cooler night air on parts farther away. Notice shadows flickering over the night landscape around you and held at bay by the flames. Imagine a long string of storytellers around this fire—storytellers of your own family and memories, and those of people on the land long before. Imagine them there with you, telling or singing or dancing their stories. Maybe some wear masks or meaningful costumes. Hear the beat of the voices, the rattles or drums, or any other sounds you associate with the sharing of family stories. Feel their energy in your DNA, in the ground beneath you, in the air you breathe that's been swirling around Earth for generations.

3. With that context and from those imaginings or memory, **answer these questions** for yourself in a journal. Consider tackling one or two at a time over a series of days. They're also good fodder for conversation with your creative community.

   - Who were the first storytellers in your life? (Some may not have been human.)
   - What in your life served as the fire? This focal point or gathering place where stories were told might include the kitchen table, a grandparent's house, or long car rides, for instance.
   - What are some of the earliest stories you can recall being told about you? These typically involve character strengths and weaknesses or roles in the family. *(For instance, "smart," "lazy," "good girl/boy," or "baby of the family.")* Often these stories are distilled from incidents or family legends—though they may say more about the people telling them than about *you.*) When did these stories first get told, or how often, and by whom?
   - In what ways has storytelling been a force for good in your life?
   - In what ways has it been a source of trouble or conflict, perhaps because of stories that involved mistaken assumptions or harmful lies?
   - Who in your early life wore a mask? How did that influence stories told by or about them?
   - What stories have you heard or invented about creativity that may not be true? *(For instance, "Artists are born, not made," "I don't have enough time," or "I'll never be good at _____.")*
   - What is the primary story you tell now about yourself? (This may revolve around your work or created family, such as "high achiever who's a good mother but clumsy.") Do you have others, too, perhaps for different audiences?
   - How do any of those stories support or limit you, particularly in creative situations?
   - What's one story about yourself or your creativity you'd like to squash or revise? *("I'm not a poet," "I produce work too slowly," or "I can't draw" are some common examples.)*
   - What's one action you could take that would change that story or prove it even slightly inaccurate? This action may involve an experiment, a class, a mentor, etc.—or simply require you to stop repeating that story to yourself.

4. **Turn your attention to a particular project and answer these questions** in your journal:

   - Who in your current project has a storyteller's role, even a small one—carrying history or shaping how the present is interpreted? This might be a place or item, not only a character. In addition, the story they're trying to tell may not be true, or not told until the end.
   - How does this storyteller relate to or interact with your main character or subject?
   - Are there multiple storytellers with competing or conflicting stories? *(For example, a parent and a teen, or two bickering friends.)* If so, who is the audience for each?
   - How is storytelling in your project a force for good or trouble? Or both?

- Who or what in your project wears a mask? Why? What kind of mask is it—part of a story they're telling themselves, or part of a story for somebody else?
- What might it take to unmask them, and what might happen then?
- Is there someone or something in your project that serves as the fire—a focal point, meeting place, or idea that brings people together or keeps the scary shadows pushed back?
- What would happen if that fire or hub is quenched or allowed to dissipate? What darkness might lunge forward? How could that increase tension in your story?
- When it comes to this particular project:
  - What shadows are lurking at the edges of your confidence?
  - What harmful stories have you told yourself about your ability to overcome them? *(For example, "This kind of work won't sell.")*
  - Identify at least one demonstrable falsehood or factual error in those harmful stories. (If you need help, creative friends or mentors can often provide it, or remember that simply because something has been true in the past does not mean it will be true forever.)
  - What more supportive story can you carry for defense as you step away from the fire and move into the creative but scary shadows? *(For instance, "Others can help me make it better" or "Every market trend is kicked off by something.")*

5. **Identify at least one way to incorporate your insights** into your creative practice or project.

Build a Better Vision Board

How this can help you: Visualizing what you want, how to get it, and, crucially, how it benefits others can enlist your subconscious to help accomplish it.

The best $4.99 I ever spent gave me access to the online software I used to create a map of the setting for my latest novel. Although I'd been working on the book for more than a year, seeing the locations and landscape on paper brought it to motivational life. It also helped me correct some logistical issues. Though I'm still struggling to get this story right, every time I see that map I get a new surge of enthusiasm.

Humans rely predominantly on visuals. The eyes deliver at least three-quarters of the sensory input processed by the average brain.[15] That's one reason developing visuals for creative work, even if you're not an illustrator or visual artist, can help you better grasp the project to move it forward.

Why this activity fits winter: *Vision is the sense most associated with winter, which is prime time for looking to the future.*

A map is a narrow example, of course. More broadly, vision boards can help you develop a specific character, spark insights about a whole project, or make general creative aspirations more concrete and therefore achievable. Making a vision board is a great way, for instance, to elaborate on a theme, intention, or "nudge" word for a new year. Try it on National Vision Board Day, which falls on the second Saturday of January.[16] You don't have to believe in any law of attraction; there's science behind deliberate goal setting and planning. Whether for a goal, a project, or a single character, a vision board can help you clarify what you want and keep your intention and enthusiasm fresh over time.

But here are two ingredients, often overlooked, that can make your vision board more potent. **First, your board must acknowledge the hard parts and risks**—the fears or failings that may get in the way, or the cost and sacrifice any achievement requires. Vision board and visualization research suggests they're effective in helping us (or characters) achieve goals by increasing motivation and confidence—but there's a catch.[17] You can't focus solely on the goal. Those who do are actually *less* likely to achieve it than if they'd never done the vision board. For a vision board to help, you have to think through the preparation, challenges, effort, actions, and sacrifices needed to reach those aspirations.

In other words, the vision board has to focus on the journey, too, not merely the destination. Otherwise, that shiny fantasy too easily replaces action toward goals. Similarly, if you're envisioning a character, the absence of struggles or mistakes might result in a story without sufficient tension or a floundering plot detached from the character's growth.

The second unusual component, which can make your vision board more motivational, is to include how achieving the goal will benefit someone else. Winter is no time to be selfish. Challenging times require pulling together for mutual benefits. So what contribution will your vision (or the character's) make to others? Acknowledging what you'll give to balance what you hope to receive can be especially helpful for those who struggle to "find time" for their creative work.

You can create an electronic vision board with apps like Pinterest or Canva, but tactile work with art supplies or collage makes it more real. The more of your senses you involve, the better for engaging your subconscious in achieving the goal.

If you're creating a vision board for a project or character, you might refer to activities you've completed in other seasons that might help, such as Find a Project Talisman, Break a Rule, or Unearth Secrets, for instance. If you're creating a vision board for a theme or "nudge" word or creative aspiration, this activity is a good follow-up to Gnaw Your Creative Bone. If you've already completed it, the answers in Spring's Connect with Your Artistic Spirit (p. 66) may help, too. Use your board to help manifest the answers and values you noted in those activities.

Build a Better Vision Board—Step by Step

You'll need: Collage supplies such as magazines, scissors, and a glue stick—or any other art supplies you enjoy—plus a large piece of paper or cardboard. Plan to spend at least 45 minutes.

1. **Assemble your materials.** Find or create a variety of images or words that express your goal or what you know about your character or project. Think creatively and symbolically; what you choose doesn't need to make sense to anyone else. Don't arrange images yet; just collect them in a pile.

2. **Find a few images or words for the shadows** involved with your topic—the flaws, hard parts, or dark side mentioned above.
    + A board for a character, for instance, ought to include flaws or failings—and what will befall them if they don't achieve their goals.
    + A board for a project needs to include something that represents your fear that it may fail or remain incomplete—and perhaps a darkness for elements you don't yet understand.
    + A theme or goal board should include images for the effort and potential sacrifice any goal or particular focus requires. (You can't focus in one area without looking away from something else.)

3. Now think about **steps you (or the character) will need to take**. *(These might include butt-in-chair work, classes, support from others, learning from a mistake, etc.)* Find or create a few words or images for each.

4. Last but not least, find or create images or words for **how the world will be better** if your vision is made manifest. Who or what does your character save, or how will your efforts, in

some small way, help others? Identify a specific reader who no longer feels alone, a way in which your work may inspire others, or a social value that will be reinforced, for instance.

5. Look through all your images and **follow your intuition to place and combine** the best and most evocative into a meaningful whole. Remember to include at least one image from each of your four piles—but if you like, put the "dark side" or effort images on the back of the vision board instead of the front.

6. Before you finish, **incorporate a wildcard image**—a blank area or question mark, for instance—that can represent the mystery of the future. No matter what you envision, the results will likely include some surprise.

7. **Post your board where you can see it** often. Let it spur you to work and cheer you during setbacks.

8. **Keep the images you selected but didn't use** in an envelope. Reviewing them over time or when you're struggling can spark new ideas or add depth to your grasp of your work or goals.

Wildly Inspired

Shine Light on Deceptions

 *How this can help you:* Reveal potential self-deception in your creative life to throw off psychological barriers to creating better work and enjoying it more.

Winter deceives. Things that look dead often aren't, while cold winds or swirling fog come to life to torment us. And who hasn't had hopes crushed by a false spring?

Snow and ice make good art supplies for nature's deceptions. I awoke one winter morning in Ohio to discover someone had invaded my yard, rolled body parts for a snowman, and then left them without stacking them up. Yet no footprints betrayed the path of the culprit. The balls were alone—and remarkably coiled. A long Internet search revealed the truth: Rarely, high winds play such tricks when no one's watching, leaving snow rollers in their wake.[18]

Why this activity fits winter: *It aligns with seasonal focus on reflection and communal support.*

Deception in our creative lives is less delightful. Unfortunately, most of us believe lies told by our own doubts or poorly informed, if well-meaning, early influencers. Lies about what we can't accomplish, aren't "good" at, or shouldn't try can seriously impede confidence and creative growth. Unchecked, they can cause full-blown Imposter Syndrome, which troubles famous artists and the rest of us alike.

That makes deception a winter theme worth exploring. Shine the season's harsh light on the truth. How might you be deceiving yourself about your creativity or work? Once you recognize potential lies, you can fact-check or test them for a more nuanced view of the truth.

One good way to start is to stop relying on our own warped perceptions. As a photograph can temper a distorted self-image, this activity can give you a more accurate snapshot to compare with your creative identity. Returning the favor for others can also broaden your appreciation of the possibilities and all our unique strengths.

Snow roller © M. Granche, Creative Commons

Shine Light on Deceptions—Step by Step

You'll need: Copies of the following page, a journal and pen, about an hour, and at least two trustworthy creative friends, critique group members, or classmates who are familiar with your work. (Avoid relying on family members.) If that seems impossible, see Step 1.

A Creativity Snapshot for _____
(your name here)

Please consider the creative work of the person named above as you're familiar with it to answer the questions below. Be honest but kind and focus on strengths. The purpose is not unearthing ways to improve. It's to see ourselves from others' perspectives.

When you think about this person's creative work and habits...

What three adjectives or descriptive words come to mind? (For example, lyrical, colorful, emotional.)

What three nouns or things come to mind? (For example, science, awards, cats.)

What mood or tone comes to mind?

What do you see as three strengths of this person's work or work habits?

What themes or recurring images, relationships, emotions, or symbols have you noticed in this person's work?

In what ways does this person's work seem to reflect their personality? Are there any ways in which it seems to contradict or complement that personality?

Is there any other well-known creative whose work comes to mind as similar in some way?

Any other thoughts or encouragement to add?

Return this form to that person. Thanks for helping!

Wildly Inspired

1. **Make multiple copies of the snapshot page** so each participant has as many copies as the total participating. For instance, if two friends will help you, you'll each need three copies, including one for yourself. Keep the original blank, since this activity can produce different results over time or with different people, and you may want a fresh perspective later. If you can't think of anyone to help, consider mining old critique notes, reviews, or instructor comments on assignments for key words you can pull into your own snapshot. If you don't even have that, you need more creative community! Go find some instead of completing this activity.

2. **Note your name on copies you give to each of your co-conspirators.** They should do the same so you each end up with a page for yourself and each of the others.

3. **Fill out one copy for yourself and one for each helper.** Be honest but kind and as objective as you can. Notice there's not much room for quality judgments. The questions are intended to get a more subtle picture of what you each alone bring to your art. Depending on your relationships, you may ask for constructive input, too, perhaps on the back of the form. But you can learn nearly as much without it.

4. **Return the completed forms** and compare the results. Most of us discover surprises that hint at mistaken or incomplete beliefs about ourselves.

5. **Answer these questions** for yourself in your journal (perhaps after discussing them together):
   - Where do the assessments agree or overlap?
   - What have others said that surprised you, or that you struggle to believe?
   - If any comments by others refer to process rather than product (such as "hardworking" or "prolific"), how much do you agree? How might that aspect of your process affect your work?
   - Which comments by others tickle your heart? Why? If you would like to agree but struggle to do so, why?
   - Which, if any, puzzle you? Why? What does it mean that you disagree or don't understand?
   - Are there traits you wish others had noted that don't appear? Why do you feel that way, and what could you do (such as experimentation or classes) to bring more of it to your work?

6. **Pick the six words, phrases, or creative traits that resonate most.** Include a few you agree with and at least one that's surprising or more aspirational. Write all six on a sticky note in a pyramid shape: the agreed, most fundamental three along the bottom, two in the middle, and an aspirational one at the top. See the example at right.

7. **Post this "truth" in your work area** where you can draw confidence or inspiration from it. Keep the snapshot pages to refer to when you need a boost or to compare with different results later.

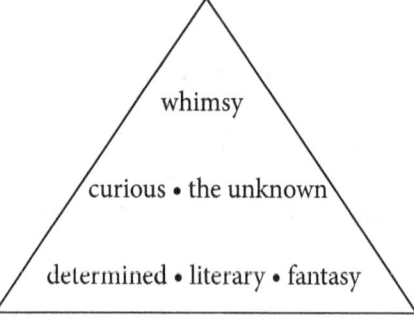

8. *Extra credit:* **Further explore this snapshot of your creativity.** For instance, jot words around each of the six points, in mind-mapping style, for associations you make with that trait or ways you could leverage it. Or list three or four ways you can emphasize your unique combination of strengths or incorporate more of the aspiration.

Fracture Your Own Fairy Tale

How this can help you: Flatten stories to types and skeletal plots to gain a new perspective on a project, especially one you're struggling with.

Once upon a time, a girl who loved to weave apprenticed herself to a famous weaver. The girl started work on a tapestry she'd seen in her dreams.

"Too many colors," said the teacher. "Rip it out and start again."

The girl tried to obey. When her teacher saw the new version, the teacher replied, "I can't tell soon enough what kind of picture this will be. Rip it out and start again."

Again, the girl tried to obey. When the teacher saw this latest version, she said, "I see—a jousting scene. Very nice. Carry on."

Unfortunately, as the girl continued to weave, a unicorn appeared in her tapestry, too. The teacher said, "What's a unicorn doing in a jousting scene? Rip it out."

The girl replied timidly, "The commotion with horses lures the unicorn in, and it's more important to me than the jousting."

But the weaver shook her head and said, "You need to learn more about weaving. Go to your room."

So the girl retreated to her cold, lonely room. She studied the ribbon in her hair, the laces in her boots, and the wick of her candle before deciding to try weaving her unicorn into something smaller: a napkin.

Why this activity fits winter: *It draws on the "bare bones" essence of the season as well as its focus on interior visualization through stories.*

With trepidation, she showed the teacher. To her surprise, the weaver loved the napkin! Unfortunately, she told the girl, "I teach people to weave tapestries, not napkins. Goodbye." With that, she turned the girl out.

The girl went home in despair. Years passed. The sun rose and rains fell. The idea she had dreamed would not go away. One day, by then an old woman, she got out the napkin and studied its design. She saw how the napkin told the same story she'd dreamed. It only needed some changes in fiber, in the warp and weft and the scale, to be appropriate for a full tapestry. She began weaving again with the napkin beside her. When she didn't know what came next, she looked at the napkin. At last she created a lovely tapestry that others admired. It had a lot of unicorn and only a wee bit of jousting. She wasn't the best weaver in all the land, but she'd successfully brought the tapestry she'd imagined into the world, and she lived well the rest of her days.

This silly tale about a tapestry and a napkin captures my experience working on a novel with a mentor. I struggled with her feedback until she suggested I write a fairy tale to drastically condense the story so I could recognize its heart and what really drove it. We both liked the fairy tale I came up with, but by then, the mentorship was over. It took time and distance, but later, I was able to complete and publish that novel with help from the insight that fairy tale provided.

I've since used this technique more than once and taught it in a workshop. Mark Twain said, "A successful book is not made of what is in it, but what is left out of it."[19] His wisdom applies to art of all kinds. Of course, knowing what to leave out can be hard to balance against the important task of making a fictional world feel authentic. Because fairy tales streamline stories to archetypes, basic emotions, and skeletal plots, they cut through some of that noise so structure and universal themes can shine through. Especially for "pantsers" like me who don't outline in advance, it's a fun way to get to the heart of the work and ensure everything else supports, rather than distracts from, that heart. This activity is fun to tackle with a creative friend or critique partner who may see that heart of your project more easily than you do; compare notes and final results.

Fracture Your Own Fairy Tale—Step by Step

You'll need: A work in progress, your imagination, a journal or computer, and a couple of hours or more.

1. **Choose a classic fairy tale opening**, from "Once upon a time" to a culture-specific opening you might know and relate to.
2. **Convert your project's protagonist into a basic, anonymous archetypal character** such as boy or girl, prince or princess, king or queen. Don't overthink it. For some stories, a more complex archetype such as magician or caregiver or wicked witch might apply. But in most cases, the basics will be easier to work with and the character's transformation—such as maturation into magician or witch—easier to track. Clarify animal stories by using a human archetype for those, too. You can give the character a name if you must, but you shouldn't need one. Remember, this is a bare-bones exercise.
3. **Place that character in a fairy-tale setting** that resonates with the setting of your project—a kingdom, a village, a deep dark wood. If you like, elaborate slightly on either the character or the setting to suggest what's not right with the scenario that will fester into a story. For instance, perhaps the king needs a wife or an heir, or the deep dark wood is inhabited by a dragon. Speaking of which:
4. **Identify an archetypal villain** to represent the antagonist in your project, though it may not appear right away. Evil rulers—or their family equivalent, evil (step)parents—wicked witches, thieves, giants and ogres, and horrible beasts can stand in for everything from mean girls to natural disasters. In your project, of course, any villain should be three-dimensional, while fairy tale villains may have understandable motives but are basically bad.
5. **Identify the desire, misfortune, or transgression that kicks off the story.** Nearly every fairy tale has at least one of these three. For instance, a grandmother gets sick, a prince wants

to inherit the kingdom, a father steals from a witch, a ball falls in a well. Think symbolically using age-old images, not modern ones. For instance, instead of a fairy tale starting with your prince hacking a computer, start with him stealing something—a more basic transgression.

6. **Identify one to three images** that will figure prominently. For instance, your hacker prince might steal the king's crown or a witch's poison. Images are what give fairy tales their power.

7. **Identify the stakes.** Think in extreme or symbolic versions of the stakes in your real story, such as imprisonment, exile, starvation, or death, as substitutes for real-world stakes like love, independence, or the emotional "starvation" of not getting what the protagonist wants.

   At this point, you should have one to three (possibly run-on) sentences like "Long ago [the fairy tale opener], a prince in a kingdom by the sea [the setting] had no interest in following the footsteps of his brute of a father but wanted instead to sail away to find his true love [the desire]. To escape his fate, one night he crept into the throne room and made off with the crown jewels [the transgression], which he planned to trade for a ship. When the king discovered the theft, he sent guards after his son with orders to execute him [the stakes]."

8. **Keep going**, keeping in mind that most fairy tales involve two failed or insufficient attempts before a successful third effort. These efforts typically get increasingly impossible and may lead to a dark moment when all seems to be lost. As best you can, create a plot arc that somehow parallels your project to ensure this work will be helpful.

9. **Introduce other characters only as absolutely necessary.** These may be a sought-after or threatened person (the true love), helpers like a fairy godmother or sidekick, a trickster who may help or hinder the hero, or a disguised adversary or agent of the villain.

10. **Incorporate repetition and a little magic** or whimsy! But keep your fairy tale to two or three pages at most. The more you can strip it down, the more it can shine light on the structure, themes, and throughline of your project.

    If you get stuck, keep in mind that many fairy tales—many narratives, period—recount these classic themes: transformations, especially coming of age, gaining independence, or recognizing one's unique gifts; overcoming hardship; restoring justice; seeing past illusion to truth; defeating evil; embracing the shadow or an Other; or finding safety in a dangerous world. Align your story with one of these to help gain a target to aim for.

11. **End by restoring harmony** somewhere (probably, though not necessarily, for your protagonist). This may look like a royal ascension, a wedding, a proper identity or role claimed or reclaimed, or another "happily ever after." This ending (if not the "all is lost" moment) may include a reversal of fortune or unexpected twist, as when the villain dies miserably in a method of their own making.

    Note: Plenty of fairy tales have unhappy endings, but they still tend to restore balance to the world of the story, if only by punishing the original transgression. Modern audiences aren't fond of such moralizing, though. A story with happiness—or at least hope—at the end is more likely to provide a useful model for your project.

Wildly Inspired

12. Read your draft aloud to yourself or your pet. Then **answer these questions** in a journal:
    - What unexpected delights does your fairy tale include? Could they have any place in your original project?
    - What aspects resonate the most emotionally for you? Are those reflected in your project in some way, or could they be?
    - What motivates your fairy tale character, and how well does that motivation align with what's in your project? Could the latter be tweaked to be stronger?
    - Is the antagonist in your project as strong or scary as the one in your fairy tale? Are there attributes of the fairy tale character you could give them without making them stereotypical?
    - Are there characters in your project that could productively be combined or eliminated?
    - Are the stakes in your project as clear as in the fairy tale? How can you heighten or clarify them?
    - Is there an image or symbol in your fairy tale that occurs in your project? If not, should there be? If so, could it be stronger or more compelling?
    - In your fairy tale, are the protagonist's efforts to succeed episodic or do they escalate? How does that compare with plot points in your project?
    - Is there a moment when all seems lost? Is there one in your project?
    - Are you aware of a classic fairy tale with parallels to the one you just created? Unless your project is a conscious retelling, this can be easier to see from your fairy tale than from your original work. If there is one, does it provide any insight into themes or meanings you might incorporate into your project?
    - What else did you notice in this process that might help you complete or improve your project? Even if it only stretched your creativity, though, it's likely to help you move forward.
13. *Extra credit:* **Write a fairy tale version of your life** or creative career (or a significant chapter of either). What does it tell you about yourself and your own heroism?

Winter Endnotes

1—See footnote 1 in the Spring section. One global Real Research survey reports a majority calling winter their favorite season, but a survey that pays respondents in Bitcoin and requires a custom cell phone app contains obvious bias toward youth. That bias is supported by multiple other survey results that suggest people younger than 24, particularly men, favor winter far more than anyone else. https://realresearcher.com/media/over-34-percent-vote-winter-as-their-most-favorite-season/

2—A few of the many studies regarding the benefits of rest on productivity and creativity: Syrek, Christine J., et al. "Well Recovered and More Creative? A Longitudinal Study on the Relationship Between Vacation and Creativity." *Frontiers in Psychology* 12: 784844. Dec. 23, 2021. https://doi.org/10.3389/fpsyg.2021.784844; Perlow, Leslie A., and Porter, Jessica L. "Making Time Off Predictable—and Required." *Harvard Business Review,* October 2009. https://hbr.org/2009/10/making-time-off-predictable-and-required; Gibson, Matthew, and Shrader, Jeffrey. "Time Use and Labor Productivity: The Returns to Sleep." *The Review of Economics and Statistics* 100:5 (2018), pp. 783-798. https://doi.org/10.1162/rest_a_00746

3—Wackermann, Jiří, et al. "Ganzfeld-Induced Hallucinatory Experience, Its Phenomenology and Cerebral Electrophysiology." *Cortex* 44:10 (2008), pp. 1364-1378. https://doi.org/10.1016/j.cortex.2007.05.003

4—Snyder, Michael. "What Do Tree Roots Do in Winter?" *Northern Woodlands*, Winter 2007. https://northernwoodlands.org/articles/article/what_do_tree_roots_do_in_winter

5—"Otherworld." *Encyclopedia of Religion.* Encyclopedia.com. June 14, 2024. https://www.encyclopedia.com

6—Liungman, Carl G. *Dictionary of Symbols* (English Edition). Santa Barbara: ABC-Clio, 1991, pp. 8-10, 109, 238, 300-302, 306-308

7—Thoreau, Henry David. Letter to Harrison Blake, March 27, 1848

8—Hanes, Michael J. "Clinical Application of the 'Scribble Technique' with Adults in an Acute Inpatient Psychiatric Hospital." *Art Therapy: Journal of the American Art Therapy Association*, 12:2, pp. 111-117, https://doi.org/10.1080/07421656.1995.10759141; Berger, L. R. "The Winnicott Squiggle Game: A Vehicle for Communicating with the School-Aged Child." *Pediatrics* 66:6 (1980), pp. 921-924; Claman, L. "The Squiggle-Drawing Game in Child Psychotherapy." *American Journal of Psychotherapy.* 34:3 (1980), pp. 414-425. https://doi.org/10.1176/appi.psychotherapy.1980.34.3.414

9—Hanes, Michael J. "Clinical Application of the 'Scribble Technique' with Adults in an Acute Inpatient Psychiatric Hospital." *Art Therapy: Journal of the American Art Therapy Association*, 12:2, pp. 111-117, https://doi.org/10.1080/07421656.1995.10759141

10—Halse Anderson, Laurie. *Speak*. New York: Farrar, Straus, and Giroux, 1999. If you're unfamiliar with it, see the Wikipedia entry at https://en.wikipedia.org/wiki/Speak_(Anderson_novel)

11—"Frozen Frogs Don't Croak." U.S. National Science Foundation, April 26, 2005. https://www.nsf.gov/news/frozen-frogs-dont-croak. The phenomenon of seeds or bulbs needing a period of cold is well known and is called cold stratification. See "Stratification (seeds)" at Wikipedia: https://en.wikipedia.org/wiki/Stratification_(seeds)

12—See https://www.nationaldaycalendar.com/national-day/national-tell-a-fairy-tale-day-february-26; https://www.press.org/special-months

13—Pagel, Mark. "Anthropology: The Long Lives of Fairy Tales." *Current Biology*, 26:7 (2016), pp. R279-R281. https://doi.org/10.1016/j.cub.2016.02.042

14—Schank, R. C., and Abelson, R. P. "Knowledge and Memory: The Real Story." *Knowledge and Memory: The Real Story*, R. S. Wyer, Jr. (Ed.), Lawrence Erlbaum Associates, 1995, pp. 1-85, https://web-archive.southampton.ac.uk/cogprints.org/636/1/KnowledgeMemory_SchankAbelson_d.html; "The Power of Storytelling to Improve Early Childhood Learning Outcomes." *LitNerd*. March 3, 2023. https://www.litnerd.com/post/the-power-of-storytelling-to-improve-early-childhood-learning-outcomes; Einam, H., Mikulincer, M., and Shachar, R. "Shedding a Light on the Teller: On Storytelling, Meaning in Life, and Personal Goals" *The Journal of Positive Psychology*, Nov. 2024, pp. 1–15. https://doi.org/10.1080/17439760.2024.2431684

15—Man, Dariusz, and Olchawa, Ryszard. "The Possibilities of Using BCI Technology in Biomedical Engineering." *Biomedical Engineering and Neuroscience*, Feb. 7, 2018. https://doi.org/10.1007/978-3-319-75025-5_4

16—National Day Calendar, https://www.nationaldaycalendar.com/

17—Travers, Mark. "A Psychologist Explains the Power of 'Vision Boarding' for Success." *Forbes*, May 29, 2024; Farber, Neil. "Throw Away Your Vision Board." *Psychology Today*, May 23, 2012. https://www.psychologytoday.com/us/blog/the-blame-game/201205/throw-away-your-vision-board-0; Rawolle, Maika, et al. "The Motivating Power of Visionary Images: Effects on Motivation, Affect, and Behavior." *Journal of Personality*, Oct. 7, 2016. https://doi.org/10.1111/jopy.12285; Voigt, J., Jais, M., and Kehr, H. "An Image of What I Want to Achieve: How Visions Motivate Goal Pursuit." *Current Psychology* 43 (2024), pp. 21658–21672. https://doi.org/10.1007/s12144-024-05943-4

18—Wikipedia. "Snow Roller." https://en.wikipedia.org/wiki/Snow_roller

19—Letter to Henry H. Rogers, April 26-28, 1897, from twainquotes.com, http://www.twainquotes.com/Book.html

Spiral Forward

Emerge. Expand. Ripen. Rest. There's no end to this cycle of seasons, to nature's creativity or yours. Although each season comes around again and again, the cycle pushes life and time forward. Your craft skills and aesthetic move forward, too, even when it may not feel that way.

In my view, creativity is an end unto itself, much like cultivating compassion, and it can become a spiritual path. Spirituality can be defined as a sense of connection with something larger than ourselves, whether that's a community, the family of our fellow creatives, the stream of human history, the divinity of a traditional faith, or the majesty of the life force and our prolific universe. Cultivating creativity through a connection with nature achieves such a connection. It can help us move in relationship with the world around us.

If you've made it this far, consider a few final reflections:

- In what ways has your awareness or understanding of the seasons, and their influence on your work and life, shifted?
- How has your perception of your own creativity expanded or changed?
- What favorite activities or concepts from this book do you expect to return to? How have they helped you?
- How do you feel now about your lowest-scoring season (or seasons) in the Seasonal Energy Tendencies activity on pp. 20–23? How about your highest-scoring season?

- How much did you notice the spirit of various archetypes—such as spring's Trickster or Rebel, summer's Explorer or sensual Lover, autumn's eerie Magician, or winter's Artist/Sage (both storytellers)—in some of the seasonal activities? Is there an archetype you identify with most as a creative? (It may not be as obvious as Artist.) If this is an area of interest to you, you may want to review the information on pp. 32–35 or see "For further exploration" below.

I hope you'll revisit the activities in this book more than once—whether "in-season" or out. They'll offer new perspectives each time, in part because you'll be a different person, with new projects or creative challenges to confront. And, of course, work on every project has its own cycles, which may not align with any external conditions. If you need inspiration, flip through the pages at random and rely on synchronicity. That seems to be part of nature, too.

For further exploration

If you've enjoyed some of the activities in this book, consider investigating these other suggested resources:

- *The Artist's Journey* by Christopher Vogler
- *Fingerpainting on the Moon* by Peter Levitt
- *Writing Wild* by Tina Welling
- Dreamwork classes or facilitated dream groups
- Mandala psychology courses or books. The Jung Society at https://jung.org is one organization that offers frequent, low-cost online classes on such topics.
- Books or classes on the use of archetypes. You can also Google, or find a basic overview by Jericho Writers at https://jerichowriters.com/12-character-archetypes-writers-guide
- Many options for exploring fairytales by Dr. Sharon Blackie at https://sharonblackie.net

Now—enough words have been spilled here. Go experience the Earth, draw inspiration from nature, and let your creativity flow. Create! Stop worrying about whether it's a good use of time, or whether anyone else will like the result. To paraphrase Shri Krishna in the *Bhagavad Gita*:

Do the work given to you, which only you can accomplish in your unique style. Neither succumb to inaction nor concern yourself with the results; that is the province of the gods.

Acknowledgments

This book wouldn't exist without the many creative friends who helped me source, test, and refine the activities here and who encouraged me to share them with others. Special thanks go to Laurie Ann Thompson, who first planted the seed and then helped tend what grew.

You all have my gratitude and wishes for many more creative adventures together.

www.ingramcontent.com/pod-product-compliance
Lightning Source LLC
Chambersburg PA
CBHW081138010526
44110CB00061B/2515